A

BED & BREAKFAST

in

ARIZONA

*almost

TONI KNAPP, EDITOR

Special Contributor

TRAVIS ILSE

THE ROCKY MOUNTAIN SERIES

SECOND EDITION

TRAVIS ILSE
PUBLISHERS

POST OFFICE BOX 583
NIWOT, COLORADO 80544

COVER PHOTOGRAPH
© Jeff Nicholas
Sierra Press, Mariposa, California

MAP BY
Trudi Peek
Seattle, Washington

PRODUCTION BY
Alan Bernhard
Argent Associates, Boulder, Colorado

PRINTED BY
Data Reproductions,
Rochester Hills, Michigan

LIBRARY OF CONGRESS CATALOGING-IN-PUBLICATION DATA

Knapp, Toni.
    Absolutely every° bed & breakfast in Arizona (° almost)
        Toni Knapp, editor: special contributor, Travis Ilse.—2nd ed.
    p. cm. — (The Rocky Mountain Series)
    Includes index.
    ISBN 1-882092-12-0
    1. Bed & Breakfast accommodations—Arizona—Guidebooks. 2. Arizona—
Guidebooks. I. Isle, Travis, 1946-. II. Title. III. Title: Absolutely every°
bed & breakfast in Arizona (°almost) IV. Series.
    TX907.3.A6K63 1992   91-21736
    647.947.9479103—dc20   CIP

Printed in the United States of America

A B C D E F 0 5 4 3 2 1

Distributed to the trade by
PUBLISHERS GROUP WEST

To Ed Abbey

Because he stood his ground and spoke his truth;

because he made us think and laugh;

because he would have hated

to see his name in a travel book,

and because he loved Arizona

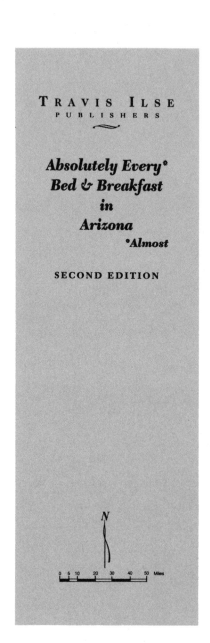

TRAVIS ILSE
PUBLISHERS

Absolutely Every*
Bed & Breakfast
in
Arizona
*Almost

SECOND EDITION

N

0 5 10   20   30   40   50 Miles

UTAH

93
Chloride

NEVADA
CALIFORNIA

Kingman

40

40

93

10

95

8

8
Yuma

Arizona

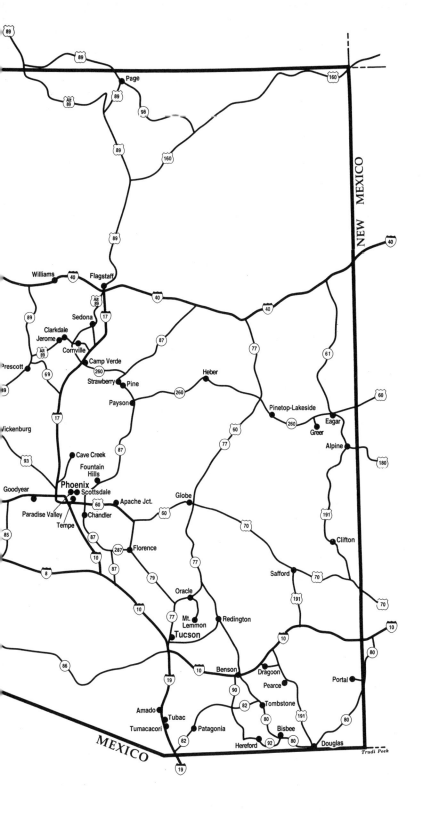

THE ROCKY MOUNTAIN SERIES

ABSOLUTELY EVERY° BED & BREAKFAST IN ARIZONA
(°ALMOST)
SECOND EDITION

ABSOLUTELY EVERY° BED & BREAKFAST
IN CALIFORNIA, MONTEREY TO SAN DIEGO
(°ALMOST)
FIRST EDITION

ABSOLUTELY EVERY° BED & BREAKFAST IN NORTHERN CALIFORNIA
(°ALMOST)
FIRST EDITION

ABSOLUTELY EVERY° BED & BREAKFAST IN COLORADO
(°ALMOST)
THIRD EDITION

ABSOLUTELY EVERY° BED & BREAKFAST IN NEW MEXICO
(°ALMOST)
REVISED EDITION

ABSOLUTELY EVERY° BED & BREAKFAST IN TEXAS
(°ALMOST)
SECOND EDITION

ABSOLUTELY EVERY° BED & BREAKFAST IN WASHINGTON
(°ALMOST)
FIRST EDITION

THE MISSISSIPPI RIVER SERIES

ABSOLUTELY EVERY° BED & BREAKFAST IN ILLINOIS
(°ALMOST)
FIRST EDITION

CONTENTS

DIRECTORY OF ARIZONA BED & BREAKFASTS

INTRODUCTION

Welcome to the second edition of *Absolutely Every° Bed & Breakfast in Arizona, (°Almost)*. We hope you have as much fun visiting the wide variety of B&Bs in Arizona as we did gathering the information for this book. As we researched and wrote this second edition we came across some fairly interesting responses to our questions, some wonderful ideas and some very inventive pet names.

Take for example an innkeeper who described the Coldstream B&B architectural style as "Non-Specific". We loved that, particularly after having to describe some B&Bs as "Territorial Adobe Ranch Haciendas," whatever that style of architecture implies. When we ask for a description of furnishings of a B&B we get the usual responses like: antique, Victorian, modern, contemporary, etc., but we liked the description of the furnishings at Cathedral Rock Lodge, "assorted comfortable."

A good number of innkeepers name their rooms after colors or local plants and animals but some innkeepers are very original. Here are some of our favorite room names in Arizona: Nautical Room at the Mine Manager House, History Room at School House Inn and Germany at Dierker House.

Breakfast descriptions are fairly routine, but there are some folks who made us curious such as the Bisbee Inn where breakfast is, "cooked to order, sit down and be served, all you can eat" or the homemade pies at Ramsey Canyon Inn where Shirley has won over 100 blue ribbons for her pies; and then there is Nancy at the Jane Cooper House who says "I choose what I want to cook." Atta girl Nancy!

We ask innkeepers to list the amenities at their B&Bs and we are often surprised by what people consider amenities. We have this ongoing argument here at the publishing house about TV, VCRs and phones in the rooms at B&B . . . it is by no means a consensus, but we generally believe that you go to a B&B to get away from these devices; however, we are amazed at the number of folks that consider these devices amenities. Anyhow here are some interesting and possibly unique amenities: the "horse motel" at Meanwhile Back at the Ranch; the solar heated stock tank at Sheps Bed & Breakfast; the "worry box" at Coldstream B&B; swimming in Oak Creek at Canyon Wren Cabins; "never a TV" at Buford House; and a flashlight in every room at Car-Mar's Southwest B&B.

To make the restriction section of each entry a little less obnoxious we have asked innkeepers to list their pets in the same section. Here are some very interesting pet names and pets in Arizona: Annie the Yorkie at The Judge Ross House is "not a yapper," Elvis the Greyhound at Gotland's Black Mountain B&B; Barkley the cat at Pinal Mountain B&B; Sneakers the terrier at Winebrenner's B&B; Happy the Queensland Heeler at Juniper Well Ranch B&B who is alleged to speak Spanish; Maggie the Norwegian Forest Cat at Briar Wreath Inn; Tricky Coyote at Tubac Country Inn comes from a "rare Chinese mother—father from a nice neighborhood"; Oink the cat at Johnstonian B&B who, "likes to eat;"

Mongoose the cat at Paz Entera B&B who catches snakes and mice; E.Z. the tortoise and Tito the iguana at Casa Tierra; and the best B&B dog name in Arizona at the Peppertrees B&B, a Lab/Retriever mix called: "Shelby Underfoot."

ARIZONA BED & BREAKFAST METHODOLOGY

This second edition of *Absolutely Every° Bed & Breakfast in Arizona (°Almost)* offers you a choice of 160 B&Bs in 44 cities, towns, villages and wide places in the road. This is the eighth book in our *Absolutely Every° Bed & Breakfast* series that includes individual books on California (Monterey to San Diego), Northern California, Colorado (Third Edition), Illinois, New Mexico, Texas (Second Edition) and Washington. There is ordering information in the back of the book.

We build our books by checking telephone directories, chambers of commerce, B&B associations, other books and tourism brochures until we have developed a relatively large list of what may or may not be B&Bs. In the case of *Absolutely Every° Bed & Breakfast in Arizona (°Almost)* we had an initial list just under 250 B&Bs from Page in the north to Douglas in the south and from Eagar in the east to Yuma in the west.

After compiling the list, we mailed a four-page survey to the innkeepers and followed up 45 days later with a reminder and another survey. When the survey came back we entered the information into our database from which we published the book. These surveys are signed by the innkeeper and kept on file with the publisher.

We received about 130 responses and from those surveys wrote 114 full entries. Then we started working the phone making about 150 phone calls to confirm or delete those B&Bs who did not respond to the survey or the reminder. Admittedly, our method of confirmation was arbitrary; we did not leave messages on answering machines; we called back later in the day and deleted the B&B if we got the answering machine a second time. If an innkeeper was rude or suspicious, we deleted them. If an innkeeper hesitated, when we asked if at the minimum, a Continental breakfast was included in the price of the room, we deleted them, and obviously, if the phone was disconnected or if there was no answer after two tries we deleted them. All in all, we made at least four attempts to contact B&Bs, i.e., survey, reminder and survey and two telephone calls.

We make an extreme effort to have the most accurate, timely and complete information in our book at press time. If we have missed a B&B let us apologize here and now. It will get into the next edition if we get a note or letter with an address on it. In fact, we love to get letters and appreciate any comments on our books or on B&Bs. Our address is Travis Ilse Publishers, PO Box 583, Niwot, CO 80544.

This gets to the reason for *(°Almost)* in our title. Given that we tentatively identified just under 250 B&Bs and could confirm 160, we have fallen short on our goal of *Absolutely Every°*. But, our decision will always be to get accurate information to our readers. If we don't have a fairly high confidence level in the existence and efficacy of a B&B, we simply don't put it in the book.

But there are other reasons for the (*Almost): Innkeepers are busy people who forget to return their survey forms with the information that gets them listed, even after a reminder or two. Innkeepers are also independent folks who may not want to be listed in any book in general, or our book in particular. Fine, be that way.

Some Reservation Service Organizations (RSOs) don't want their client B&Bs listed with information that could allow a traveler to call the B&B directly, thus endangering the RSO's commission; kind of small-time thinking, but ours is not to wonder why. If any B&B represented by an RSO wishes to be in the next edition please write us. We simply need an innkeeper's name and the address to include the B&B, using the RSO's phone number is fine with us.

Some homestays are located in areas that are zoned for residential use only. These homestays are frowned on by the local bureaucrats (and sometimes neighbors). To have information widely disseminated by a book might cause legal problems for these homestay innkeepers.

And then there is the "Goathead Factor "where someone has been rude or arrogant on the phone. If they are rude to us, there's a chance that they'll be rude to you. Here we exercise our right under the First Amendment to take them off the list and out of the database.

CAVEATS

(1) Because of the breadth of coverage of our books, we depend on the honesty of the innkeepers. We know as a fact that these are some of the most hard working, interesting and nicest people in the world. We deeply admire their work. But there is always the exception. Please write us if an innkeeper has treated you badly or misrepresented their inn.

(2) No one at Travis Ilse Publishers benefits in any way from the B&Bs in this book. We don't accept free rooms or request or receive payment for entries in the book. This book is a service to our readers, not the Arizona bed and breakfast industry; *no Innkeeper ever pays anything to be listed in the book.*

(3) The bed and breakfast industry is volatile; openings, closings and changes in prices and ownership occur regularly. That is why it is always advisable to call ahead and ask questions before you make reservations. Dropping in is chancy and seldom welcome.

(4) We wish to make it perfectly clear that the editor, contributors and Travis Ilse Publishers make no warranty, implied or specific, about operations or policies of bed and breakfast establishments, or trade associations mentioned in this book.

BED & BREAKFAST DEFINITIONS

Our guide is essentially an annotated database of small and medium-sized bed and breakfast inns, hotels and host homes that include a proper breakfast in the price of the room. However, we have exercised our right as editors, writers and data entry people to be inconsistent by including a few "grand "inns with more than 50 rooms (our maximum) because we felt their location and quality warranted inclusion. Though neither absolutely concise nor agreed upon by everyone in the industry, the following definitions may help you determine differences between types of establishments in order of size.

HOST HOME (or Homestay): The original B&B. Here the resident owner rents from one to three spare bedrooms, typically with shared bathroom, although private bathrooms are becoming more common. With professionalism and competition on the rise, host homes can offer the best of all worlds in terms of rates, services and personal touches.

GUESTHOUSE: A separate unit — cabin, carriage house, etc. Breakfast is either served in the main house or delivered to the guest house. Sometimes B&Bs have a guesthouse in addition to rooms in the main building. Clearly, these are the most private of B&B accommodations.

INN: The largest and fastest growing category in the B&B industry — five to fifteen rooms, generally with private bathrooms, larger staff and outstanding hospitality.

COUNTRY INN: Usually located in the "country" — rural areas far from the maddening crowd. Rooms number between five and twenty-five and a restaurant or dining hall serves other meals besides breakfast.

HOTEL: Usually small or historic hotels between twenty-five and fifty rooms, that have been renovated to preserve their historic past and charm.

LODGE OR WORKING RANCH: A country inn located in a resort or remote area. While breakfast is always included in the price of the room, often, complete meal packages are offered.

OUR GUIDEBOOK DEFINITIONS

Our guide is organized in a clear, friendly format that avoids codes, symbols and endless narrative. Our goal is provide you with more information than you need to make an informed decision about a B&B and ask the right questions when you call for reservations. Each town for which there are complete B&B listings is covered with a thumbnail sketch of information on sights, festivals and strange, little-known facts followed by brief instructions on how to get there.

In addition to 114 survey-based listings, there are 46 short listings that include the B&B name, address, telephone number, innkeeper's name and sometimes a KUDO/COMMENT. These listings are based on a telephone conversation where the person answering the phone confirmed that the number called was a functioning B&B and that breakfast is included in the price of the meal. For these short listings, no one signed a survey warranting that all the information was correct. We assume honesty on the part of the innkeepers; but *always call first*.

The B&B name is set in large type followed by the address, telephone number, toll-free number, FAX number, and names of the innkeepers and languages other than English spoken by the staff. Note that there are some towns in Arizona where the post office does not deliver to street addresses. Always ask the innkeeper for a mailing address; never assume that mailing to an address in the book will get your deposit to the B&B.

Digression #1 . . . 800 numbers followed with cute words, e.g., 800-INN-FOOL. One of the worst marketing ideas ever, because it is inconvenient to look for all those letters on the key pad. In fact, wasn't it the THE TELEPHONE COMPANY in the '50s that changed all the old word exchanges to numbers for just that reason. Dumb, stupid, a waste of time and inconvenient for B&B guests. By the way, there are digressions throughout the book that are always marked by ellipses followed by initials (...TI). Most of these come from Travis himself on the final edit, but a good number come from the editor, the data entry person, or the production type.

LOCATION: Where the B&B actually is relative to the town or area it is in (i.e., directions and miles from the center of town, a highway exit or nearest landmark). It's a good idea to carry the book along with you or keep the B&B telephone number in your daybook just in case you are direction-impaired.

OPEN: Most B&Bs in Arizona are open all year, but there are some seasonal B&Bs, particularly in the mountains and backcountry. Note that some B&Bs close for a week or two randomly when the Innkeeper decides that someplace else like Aspen or Abaco sounds like a pretty good idea.

DESCRIPTION: On our survey form that the Innkeeper completes for this book, we ask when a building was built, the architectural style, type of furnishing and whether it is on the Arizona or National Historic Registers. With this book we have let some notes on landscaping and surroundings slip in here. Tell us if this helps in your decision.

NUMBER OF ROOMS: This is a notation of the rooms with private bathrooms and with shared bathrooms. Also noted here are the availability of suites and guesthouses that are assumed to have private bathrooms, *but always ask*. We also ask the innkeepers to name a favorite room. While it is not surprising that the room named is often the most expensive room in the house, it is usually a very special room with extra amenities, such as a tub for two and a terrific view.

RATES: This may be the most confusing section of our book, simply because there is no standard in the B&B industry for setting rates. We have simply tried to reprint the innkeeper's range of rates that vary by private or shared bathroom, season and rooms. Use the rates in the book as a guideline only. Ask the innkeeper for a specific rate for a specific room. Ask about lower mid-week rates, extended stay rates, seniors' rates. There are some very good deals out there. We also note minimum stay requirement and cancellation policies. Digression # 2 . . . Innkeepers need the protection of cancellation policies, but anything more than two week's notice for a full refund is just dumb. Charging a fee to process a cancellation seems spiteful. Excessive cancellation policies and fees for cancellation are counterproductive to the Bed & Breakfast industry.

BREAKFAST: The second most important reason (think about it) for staying in a B&B is the breakfast that is *always* included in the price of the room. So we ask the innkeepers for an accurate description of their morning fare: a *full breakfast* ranges from the familiar eggs, pancakes, meats, fruits and beverages to three courses formally served, to a full buffet. *Continental* is usually fresh coffee, fruit, fresh juices and assorted baked goodies, usually homemade; *Continental Plus* is somewhere in between, more than Continental and less than a full breakfast. Digression # 3 . . . We are seeing more and more "B&Bs" just offer a loaded refrigerator instead of a real breakfast. This makes us wonder when some motel is going to offer a certificate for breakfast burritos at the the local jiffy mart and then try to call itself a B&B.

CREDIT CARDS: Whether or not credit cards are accepted is listed here. But be prepared—bring a checkbook or travelers checks. Some B&Bs do not accept credit cards because the local bank is run by morons or because of the added expense to the innkeeper. Note also that some innkeepers will accept credit cards for a reservation conformation only but not for payment when you check-out.

AMENITIES: All the "extras "that make a B&B vastly different from other accommodations. These may include: a hot tub, fireplaces, afternoon wine and cheese, nature trails, a llama petting zoo. . . .

RESTRICTIONS: Things that you can't do or bring to a B&B that usually involve smoking, children and pets.

Most B&Bs do not allow smoking inside the establishment, although a good number have outside smoking areas.

Children are problematical. While some B&Bs welcome them, others do not; and most set an age limit. Be considerate. If you take your children to a B&B make sure that they are under voice command. One Colorado Innkeeper said it best, "Children of responsible parents are always welcome."

A good number of B&Bs have resident pets and would rather not have dog fights every time a guest rolls up with a pack of Basset Hounds in the back of his Lincoln; so leave your dog at the kennel. We also list the names of resident pets because we believe that pets are an integral part of a home away from home and good fun to have around. Not to worry if you are allergic to pets as most Innkeepers do not allow their pets in the guest rooms.

A good rule is to always ask about restrictions when you call for a reservation.

AWARDS: Any awards given an inn that are recognized and significant to the hospitality industry or historic preservation organizations.

REVIEWED: Books in which a B&B has been reviewed. We have made an effort to include only those B&B books that are truly "review" publications where the writer and publisher receive no compensation of any kind (including free rooms and meals) for their review.

Digression # 4 . . . Fee-based bed & breakfast books . . . while no one really cares about the standards of another industry, there is a clear distinction in book publishing between the author and publisher who assume all risks for a book and the author or publisher who solicit a fee for including a B&B in a book, the former is called publishing, the latter is called advertising.

RATED: Indicates whether a B&B has been rated by the American Automobile Association, American Bed & Breakfast Association or Mobil Travel Guides. These ratings are a good indication of the quality of a B&B, *but* because a B&B is not rated is meaningless. There are many great B&Bs that are not rated.

MEMBER: Membership in professional associations recognized by the hospitality industry.

KUDOS/COMMENTS: These are comments from other innkeepers and inveterate B&B guests. We welcome your comments too; write us at Travis Ilse Publishers, PO Box 583, Niwot, CO 80544.

Bed & Breakfast Associations

Trade associations are not reservations services, although many do make direct reservations. Normally, a true trade association is a non profit organization whose principal purpose is help promote its member B&Bs.

National Bed & Breakfast Associations

American Bed & Breakfast Association
1407 Huguenot Road
Midlothian, VA 23113
804-379-2222

Association of American Historic Inns
PO Box 336
Dana Point, CA 92629
714-496-6953

National Bed & Breakfast Association
PO Box 332
Norwalk, CT 06851
203-847-6196

Professional Association of Innkeepers International
PO Box 90710
Santa Barbara, CA 93190
805-965-0707

Tourist House Association
RD 2, Box 355A
Greentown, PA 18426
717-857-0856

Formal Rating Systems

American Automobile Association
1000 AAA Drive
Heathrow, FL 32746

American Bed & Breakfast Association
1407 Huguenot Road
Midlothian, VA 23113

Mobil Travel Guides
PO Box 7600
Chicago, IL 60680

Dear Traveler:

As you visit B&Bs you leave with opinions, particularly from the great B&Bs where the room was perfect, the innkeepers wonderful and the food beyond description.

We'd like to hear your thoughts on any B&B that you visit. Just copy the form on the following page and fold a bunch of them into the book so that they'll be handy when you travel. If you give us permission to use some or all of your comments in the next edition of this book, we'll send you a free copy of this or any other books in the series (AZ, CA, Northern CA, CO, IL, NM, TX, WA).

Let us know what you think. Write to us at Travis Ilse Publishers, PO Box 583, Niwot, CO 80544. We love to get letters.

—Travis Ilse   —Toni Knapp

B&B GUEST COMMENT CARD

B&B VISITED: _____

LOCATION: _____

DATES VISITED: _____

COMMENTS, KUDOS, QUIBBLES: _____

_____

_____

_____

_____

_____

❏ I/we grant Travis Ilse Publishers permission to incorporate some or all of our comments in future editions of this book.

❏ I/we prefer not to be quoted, but here are our comments anyway.

NAME_____ DATE _____

ADDRESS (CITY, STATE, ZIP)_____

_____ PHONE _____

Please mail to: Travis Ilse (AZ2), PO Box 583, Niwot, CO 80544

B&B GUEST COMMENT CARD

B&B VISITED: _____

LOCATION: _____

DATES VISITED: _____

COMMENTS, KUDOS, QUIBBLES: _____

_____

_____

_____

_____

_____

❏ I/we grant Travis Ilse Publishers permission to incorporate some or all of our comments in future editions of this book.

❏ I/we prefer not to be quoted, but here are our comments anyway.

NAME_____ DATE _____

ADDRESS (CITY, STATE, ZIP)_____

_____ PHONE _____

Please mail to: Travis Ilse (AZ2), PO Box 583, Niwot, CO 80544

AJO

A small desert oasis and inactive copper mining town, 42 miles south of Gila Bend and 10 miles northwest of Why via Highway 85. On the eastern edge of Cabeza Prieta National Wildlife Refuge and 12 miles north of the amazing Organ Pipe Cactus National Monument. Check out the New Cornelia Open Pit Mine.

THE GUEST HOUSE INN

3 Guest House Road, Ajo, AZ 85321   520-387-6133
Norma & Mike Walker, Resident Owners
Spanish spoken

LOCATION	At the only traffic light turn south on La Mina Avenue. Turn right at the sign for the inn and right again at another sign that will be Guest House Road.
OPEN	All year
DESCRIPTION	1925 Southern Plantation with Southwestern furnishings.
NO. OF ROOMS	Four rooms with private bathrooms. The Old Pueblo Room is the best.
RATES	High season, September through May, rates are $69 for a single or a double with a private bathroom. Off season, June through August, rates for a single or a double with a private bathroom are $59. There is no minimum stay and cancellation requires 24 hours notice before the posted check-out time of 2 p.m.
CREDIT CARDS	Diners Club, MasterCard, Visa
BREAKFAST	Full breakfast is served in the dining room and includes pecan waffles topped with cream, bacon, sausage, eggs, toast, muffins, fresh fruit, coffee, tea and orange juice.
AMENITIES	Separate heating and cooling, tub/shower combination, TV and fireplace in the living room and birding on the property. All rooms open onto glass-in porches.
RESTRICTIONS	No smoking, no pets.
MEMBER	Arizona Association of Bed & Breakfast Inns, Arizona Hotel & Motel Association
RATED	AAA 3 Diamonds

THE MINE MANAGER'S HOUSE INN BED & BREAKFAST

1 Greenway Drive, Ajo, AZ 85321
Jean & Micheline Fournier, Resident Owners

520-387-6505
800-266-7829
FAX 520-387-6508

LOCATION	From Highway 85, turn south at the plaza traffic light and go four blocks. Turn right and follow directions to the top of the hill and through the gate.
OPEN	All year
DESCRIPTION	1919 Craftsman with a mixture of antique and modern furnishings.
NO. OF ROOMS	Five rooms with private bathrooms. Pick the Nautical Room.
RATES	Year-round rates for single or a double with a private bathroom are $69 to $105. There is no minimum stay, cancellation requires three days notice.
CREDIT CARDS	Visa
BREAKFAST	Full breakfast served in dining room includes fresh fruit or juice, "famous" eggs benedict, "secret recipe" strawberry waffles and tea and coffee.
AMENITIES	Hot tub, reading room, patio with BBQ grill, fireplace, gourmet ice cream in the evening, 30 mile view and limited handicapped access.
RESTRICTIONS	No smoking, no pets, "there is a B&B for pets in Ajo." and no children.
REVIEWED	*American Historic Inns*
RATED	AAA 3 Diamonds, Mobil 3 Stars
KUDOS/COMMENTS	"Unique setting and home on the desert."

AMADO

Located in near the border on I-19, 35 miles south of Tucson. Great birding country just west of the Madera Recreation Area.

REX RANCH

131 East Amado Montosa Road, Amado, AZ 85645   *520-398-2914*
Richard & Barbara Blake, Resident Owners

KUDOS/COMMENTS "Lovely and very southwestern."

APACHE JUNCTION

At the junction of Highways 60, 89 and 88, 35 miles east of Phoenix in the foothills of the Superstition Mountains. February is busy with the Lost Dutchman Days Festival and the 16th Century Renaissance Festival, a medieval celebration. Check out the Goldfield Ghost Town and Mine Tours.

MEANWHILE BACK AT THE RANCH– SUPERSTITION MT. B&B

6300 E. Pioneer Street, Apache Junction, AZ 85219   *602-982-2112*
Joy Bishop, Resident Owners   *800-570-2112, ext. 2*

LOCATION	Five miles northeast of town via Highway 88. Right on Superstition Boulevard, left on Mountain View Road, right on Pioneer Street and right again at Ranch.
OPEN	October through June
DESCRIPTION	1950 Territorial ranch cabins with antique furnishings.
NO. OF ROOMS	Three cabins with private bathrooms & kitchens.
RATES	Seasonal rates for a single or a double with a private bathroom are $79 to $100. There is no minimum stay and cancellation requires thirty days notice for longer-term stays.
CREDIT CARDS	MasterCard, Visa
BREAKFAST	Continental Plus is served in a basket at the door of the cabin. Other meals available with advance notice.
AMENITIES	Radio in rooms, phone in lodge, fireplaces, complimentary refreshments. "Horse Motel", stables available for overnight boarding of horses, wedding chapel and outdoor facilities for western parties for up to 150 people.
RESTRICTIONS	None

BENSON

Originally a railroad center, Benson is located 42 miles east of Tucson on I 10. Visit the nearby Cochise Stronghold or hop a train for the San Pedro River Ride.

REDINGTON LAND & CATTLE CO.
CASCABEL RANCH

HC1, Box 730, Benson, AZ 85602   520-212-5555
Don Steinman & Barbara Litton, Resident Owners

LOCATION	Take I-10 to exit 306, go north through Pomerene on Pomerene Road. Continue 23 miles after the road turns to dirt to mile post 24. Ranch headquarters are 1/2 mile on the left.
OPEN	All year
DESCRIPTION	An early 1900s Territorial ranch house, guest house and bunk house with cowboy furnishings, located on a working ranch of 3,600 acres.
NO. OF ROOMS	One room with a private bathroom and two rooms share two bathrooms. Pick the guesthouse.
RATES	Year-round rates for a single or a double with a private bathroom are $75. The bunkhouse rents for $10 a bunk with your own bunkroll and an additional $10 for a bunkroll if you don't have one. Reservation are must with a 50% deposit. If you cancel, the deposit is refunded if the rooms are rented, otherwise credit is issued for a future stay.
CREDIT CARDS	No
BREAKFAST	Continental Plus is served in the dining room or outdoors and includes juice, fruit, hot and cold cereal, ranch-baked breads (zucchini, banana, cranberry, white, brown, etc.) local jellies and preserves. Special meals, lunch and dinner are available.
AMENITIES	Hot tub, horseback riding, guided hiking tours, facilities available for guests' horses, cattle drives, pack trips, "whatever you need."
RESTRICTIONS	No pets. There are five dogs, 15 cats, 30 horses, 50 cows and three goats on the property.

ZR HEREFORD RANCH

PO Box 2225, Benson, AZ 85602   520-586-3509
Peggy Monzingo, Resident Owner   FAX 520-586-3509

LOCATION	About 10 miles east of Benson. Call for directions.
OPEN	All year
DESCRIPTION	A 1900-1942 adobe cattle ranch headquarters.
NO. OF ROOMS	Two rooms with private bathrooms
RATES	High season, November through March, rates for a single or a double with a private bathroom are $65 to $75. Off season, April through October, rates for a single or a double with a private bathroom are $50 to $60. There is no minimum stay and there is a cancellation policy.
CREDIT CARDS	No
BREAKFAST	Full breakfast is served in the dining room and is "guest's choice." Lunch and dinner are also available as are picnic lunches and cookouts.
AMENITIES	Hiking tours over the ranch, tea, coffee and popcorn, fruit in season, "we do not provide horses, but guest are welcome to go with us when we do various ranch activities."
RESTRICTIONS	No pets.

BISBEE

This mile-high copper-mining boomtown with fine Victorian homes lies 95 miles southeast of Tucson via I-100 & Highway 80, just 10 miles north of the U.S./Mexico border. The Ramsey Canyon Wildlife Preserve is a hummingbird-watcher's paradise. Check out the Lavender Open Pit & Copper Queen Mine. Summer's fun annual events include the Vuelta de Bisbee bicycle race; the 26-mile Mule Mountain Marathon; May to September wine festivals.

THE BISBEE GRAND HOTEL

61 Main Street, Bisbee, AZ 85603   *520-432-5900*
Bill Thomas, Resident Owner

LOCATION	Downtown Old Bisbee.
OPEN	All year
DESCRIPTION	1906 two-story Victorian Box hotel with saloon and antique furnishings; listed on the State Historic Register.
NO. OF ROOMS	Seven rooms with private bathrooms and four rooms share a bathroom. The suites are recommended by Bill.
RATES	Year-round rates for a single or a double with a private bathroom are $65 to $75 and a single or a double with a shared bathroom is $50. The suites are $95 and the entire hotel rents for $845.22. There is no minimum stay and cancellation requires 48 hours notice.
CREDIT CARDS	Amex, Discover, MasterCard, Visa
BREAKFAST	Full breakfast is served in the dining area and includes an egg dish, meat, fruits, Danish, coffee and juice.
AMENITIES	Western saloon equipped with 110 year old back bar fixture plus billiards room.
RESTRICTIONS	No smoking, no pets, no children
RATED	AAA 2 Diamonds, Mobile 2 Stars

THE BISBEE INN

45 O.K. St., Bisbee, AZ 85603   *520-432-5131*
Jill Thomas, Manager
French spoken

LOCATION	Take "Tourist Information" exit into Bisbee. At first stop sign just go straight up the hill on O.K. Street.
OPEN	All year, closed in June
DESCRIPTION	1917 two-story restored brick Western boarding house with antique furnishings; on the National and State Historic Registers.
NO. OF ROOMS	One suite with private bathroom and 17 rooms share 12 bathrooms. Pick the suite.
RATES	High season, December 26 through May 31, rates are $69 for the suite and $33 to $43 for a single or a double with a shared bathroom. Off season, July 1 through December 24, rates are $4 less. There is no minimum stay and cancellation requires 24 hours notice.
CREDIT CARDS	MasterCard, Visa
BREAKFAST	Full "cooked to order, sit down and be served, all you can eat" eggs, bacon, cereal, pancakes, toast, potatoes, fruit salad, juice, coffee and tea, all served in the dining room.
AMENITIES	TV room & lobby.
RESTRICTIONS	No smoking.
MEMBER	Professional Association of Innkeepers International

THE CLAWSON HOUSE

116 Clawson Avenue, Bisbee, AZ 85603   520-432-5237
Wally Kuehl & Jim Grosskopf, Resident Owners   800-467-5237

KUDOS/COMMENTS   "Beautiful antiques tastefully used and displayed. You feel like you
are in an aerie at the Clawson House because it sits on a hill
overlooking Bisbee, great innkeepers." ... "Beautiful setting - lovely
furniture - friendly hosts - good breakfast."... "Wonderfully eclectic
B&B, interesting innkeepers and great location."

CURRY HOME BED & BREAKFAST

608 Powell Street, Bisbee, AZ 85603   520-432-4815
Joy & John Timbers, Resident Owners

LOCATION   In the Warren Section of Bisbee. Take Highway 80 past Old Bisbee
to the traffic circle (about 1.5 miles). Take the second exit marked
(H) for Hospital and Bisbee Road and go to Hospital (one mile) turn
left on Cole at the Hospital follow Cole to Powell (.5 mile). The
B&B is on the corner of Cole and Powell.

OPEN   All year

DESCRIPTION   A 1906 two-story Spanish mission style with Victorian furnishings;
listed on the State Historic Register.

NO. OF ROOMS   Two rooms with private bathrooms and four rooms share two
bathrooms. Pick the Beige room.

RATES   Year-round rates for a single or a double with a private bathroom are
$65 to $70 and a single or a double with a shared bathroom are $60.
There is no minimum stay and there is a cancellation policy.

CREDIT CARDS   MasterCard, Visa

BREAKFAST   "Fabulous" full breakfast is served in the dining room includes juice,
coffee, tea, rolls, fresh fruit salad, pancakes, bacon, eggs, hash
browns, French toast, cereal, crepes filled with scrambled eggs,
quiche and Jay's eggs benedict.

AMENITIES   Music room with Baby Grand Piano and TV, refreshments in
afternoon and evenings, patios.

RESTRICTIONS   No smoking. There are two "precious" cats and one "precious" dog
that are housed separately from the guests.

REVIEWED   *America's Wonderful Little Hotels & Inns*

THE GREENWAY HOUSE

401 Cole Avenue, Bisbee, AZ 85603   520-432-7170
George S. Knox and Joy O'Clock, Resident Owners   800-253-3325
Spanish spoken   FAX 520-432-7917

LOCATION	Highway 80 south past Old Bisbee, right on Bisbee Road & left on Cole.
OPEN	All year
DESCRIPTION	1906 restored two-story Craftsman with antique furnishings.
NO. OF ROOMS	Eight rooms with private bathrooms.
RATES	Year-round rates for a single or a double with a private bathroom are $75 to $85 and the suites are $100 to $125. There is a two day minimum stay and cancellation requires 72 hours notice.
CREDIT CARDS	MasterCard, Visa.
BREAKFAST	Continental Plus is served in guest rooms and includes fruit cups, two juices, English muffins, cereals, coffee, tea, hot chocolate, blueberry muffins. Special meals are available for groups by prior arrangement.
AMENITIES	Flowers, robes, hair dryer, billiard room, patio with BBQ and fire ring, handicapped access.
RESTRICTIONS	No smoking, no pets
MEMBER	Arizona Bed & Breakfast Association, Bisbee Lodging Association
RATED	AAA 3 Diamonds

THE INN AT CASTLE ROCK

112 Tombstone Canyon, Bisbee, AZ 85603   520-432-4449
Donna Burgos, Manager   800-566-4449
Spanish spoken

LOCATION	Take I-10 south to the Benson Cutoff to Bisbee. Take Highway 90 through Mule Pass tunnel, get off at 1st off ramp into Bisbee, travel down Tombstone Canyon, the inn is the four story building on the right.
OPEN	All year
DESCRIPTION	An 1890s four-story miner's boarding house with a variety of decors.
NO. OF ROOMS	16 rooms with private bathrooms and one room shares one bathroom. Pick the Cardinal Room.
RATES	Year-round rates for a single or a double with a private bathroom are $40 to $60, and $40 for a single or a double with a shared bathroom. The suites start at $60. There is a two night minimum on holiday weekends and cancellation is by noon of the day of arrival.
CREDIT CARDS	MasterCard, Visa
BREAKFAST	Full breakfast is served buffet style in the dining room or outside during the summertime and includes eggs, bacon, homemade banana bread, varied muffins, different cereals, coffee, tea, juice, milk, yogurt, fresh fruit plates, toast. Dinner and lunch are available in the restaurant.
AMENITIES	Glass of wine in the evening, pyramid room for TV,
RESTRICTIONS	No smoking except outside or on the balconies, no pets, all children are welcome.

THE JUDGE ROSS HOUSE

605 Shattuck Street, Bisbee, AZ 85603   520-432-4120
Jim & Bonnie Douglass, Resident Owners

LOCATION	East on Highway 80 past Old Bisbee, continue on 1.2 miles to traffic circle and exit on road that says "to Warren Hospital". Go six blocks and turn east on Cole Avenue, continue to stop sign on Arizona Street and go through the stop sign to dead end, turn right, first house on the right.
OPEN	All year (Closed July 2 through 4 and December 23 and 26) but may make exceptions.
DESCRIPTION	1908 two-story Victorian brick with antique furnishings.
NO. OF ROOMS	One room with a private bathroom and two rooms share one bathroom. Pick the blue and white room.
RATES	Year-round rates for a single or a double with a private bathroom are $60 to $65. A single or a double with as shared bathroom is $55 to $60. There is a two day minimum stay for the room with the private bathroom and cancellation requires seven days notice.
CREDIT CARDS	MasterCard, Visa
BREAKFAST	Full breakfast is served in dining room, guest room, patio or sun porch includes eggs benedict, Dutch pancakes or Belgian waffles with fresh fruit, muffins, meats and sometimes potatoes. Special meals by arrangement.
AMENITIES	All rooms have fresh flowers, candies and telephones, TV and VCR in room with private bathroom, sun porch has a refrigerator.
RESTRICTIONS	No smoking, no pets, no children. The resident Yorkshire Terrier is called Annie and she is, "Not a yapper."
REVIEWED	*Bed & Breakfast USA*
MEMBER	Bisbee Bed & Breakfast Association, Arizona Bed & Breakfast Association
KUDOS/COMMENTS	"Very beautifully decorated home."

MAIN STREET INN

26 Main Street, Bisbee, AZ 85603   520-432-5237
Wally Kuehl & James Grosskopf, Resident Owners   800-467-5237

MILE HIGH COURT BED & BREAKFAST

901 Tombstone Canyon, Bisbee, AZ 85603   520-432-4636
Janus & Karen Poppe, Resident Owners

LOCATION	Located on the east side of the Mule Mountain Tunnel about one mile from the center of town in Tombstone Canyon.
OPEN	All year
DESCRIPTION	1884 ranch adobe located on three acres.
NO. OF ROOMS	Four suites with private bathrooms and kitchens.
RATES	Year-round rates for a single or a double are $30 to $50.
CREDIT CARDS	Discover, MasterCard, Visa
BREAKFAST	Continental breakfast is served in the suites and includes muffins, Danish, coffee, tea or cocoa.
AMENITIES	Rose garden, TV, handicapped access.
RESTRICTIONS	None. Assorted resident pets include dog, doves, ducks, chickens and peacocks, "kind of a children's zoo."
AWARDS	Best B&B in Arizona, Arizona Farm Bureau Federation

THE OLIVER HOUSE

26 Soules, Bisbee, AZ 85603   520-432-4286
Dennis Schranz, Resident Owner

PARK PLACE BED & BREAKFAST

200 East Vista, Bisbee, AZ 85603   *520-432-3054*
Bob & Janet Watkins, Resident Owners   *800-388-4388*
                                                     FAX 520-459-7603

LOCATION	Take Highway 80 around Old Bisbee to traffic circle, go half way around traffic circle and turn off on Bisbee Road. Take Bisbee Road to Congdon, go to East Vista and turn left, the B&B is mid-street on the right.
OPEN	All year
DESCRIPTION	1908 two-story Mediterranean with modern and antique furnishings.
NO. OF ROOMS	Two rooms with private bathrooms and two rooms share one bathroom. Pick the Pink Room.
RATES	Year round rates for a single or a double with a private bathroom are $40 to $50. There is no minimum stay and cancellation requires 48 hours notice.
CREDIT CARDS	Amex, MasterCard, Visa
BREAKFAST	Full four-course gourmet breakfast is served in the dining room. Catering available.
AMENITIES	Outdoor garden facilities available for special events, library and sun room.
RESTRICTIONS	No smoking, no pets (resident cat), no children.
MEMBER	Arizona Association of Bed & Breakfast Inns
RATED	Mobile 2 Stars
KUDOS/COMMENTS	"Excellent breakfasts, informal atmosphere." … "Charming older home, friendly hosts."

School House Inn Bed & Breakfast

818 Tombstone Canyon, Bisbee, AZ 85603
Marc & Shirl Negus, Resident Owners

520-432-2006
800-537-4333
FAX 520-432-2996

LOCATION	From downtown Bisbee follow Main Street 1.4 miles uphill (west). Main Street becomes Tombstone Canyon.
OPEN	All year
DESCRIPTION	A 1917 two-story brick school house with balcony.
NO. OF ROOMS	Nine rooms with private bathrooms. Marc recommends the History or Writing rooms … Great idea for naming rooms, much more interesting than the lavender suite or heartsong (argh!)…TI
RATES	Year-round rates for a single or a double with a private bathroom are $45 to $55 and the suite is $65. The entire inn rents for $500 and can house up to 25 guests. There is no minimum stay and cancellation requires 48 hours notice.
CREDIT CARDS	Amex, Diners Club, Discover, MasterCard, Visa
BREAKFAST	Full breakfast is served in the dining room includes one of several entrees such as French toast, pancakes, Southwest crustless quiche, fruit, juices, coffee and tea.
AMENITIES	Common balcony overlooking the canyon, shaded patio under 100 year old oak tree full of hummingbirds in the spring, summer and fall, private off-street parking.
RESTRICTIONS	No smoking, no pets, children over 13 are welcome.
REVIEWED	*Fodor's - The Southwest*
MEMBER	Professional Association of Innkeepers International, American Bed & Breakfast Association
KUDOS/COMMENTS	"The rooms are spacious & charmingly decorated to match the school house period." … "Very warm and friendly people with good breakfast."

White House of Warren

800 Congdon Avenue, Bisbee, AZ 85603
Edie Dortch, Resident Owner

520-432-7215

CAMP VERDE

Seventy miles north of Phoenix on I-17

B's B&B

94 Coppinger Street, Camp Verde, AZ 86322   520-567-6215
Beatrice Richmond, Resident Owner

CAVE CREEK

In the foothills, about 30 miles north of downtown Phoenix, via I-17 and Highway 74. Check out Pioneer Arizona Museum and fishing in Bartlett and Horseshoe Lakes.

ANDORA CROSSING

6434 Military Road, Cave Creek, AZ 85331   *602-488-3747*
Karen Douglass, Resident Owner

LOCATION	One city block south of Cave Creek Road on School House Road which bends left or east to become Military Road.
OPEN	October 1 through June 30.
DESCRIPTION	A 1920s ranch and guesthouse with guest ranch furnishing located on 2.5 acres.
NO. OF ROOMS	Two rooms with private bathrooms and two rooms share one bathroom. There will be four rooms with private bathrooms by 1996.
RATES	Year-round rate for a single or a double with a private bathroom is $100, the guesthouse rents for $135. There is no minimum stay and there is a cancellation policy.
CREDIT CARDS	MasterCard, Visa
BREAKFAST	Full breakfast is served in the dining room and includes "Nouveau-Cowboy" fresh fruit, granola, biscuits, ranch eggs, "and whatever else I invent." ...Nouveau-Cowboy is good enough for us...TI...Yahoo Bubba.
AMENITIES	Down comforters, pistachios and bubble bath in the room. Phone in the main house.
RESTRICTIONS	No pets, children over 12 are welcome. The Border Collie is called Honey.
REVIEWED	Just opened in 1995.

D-RAILED RANCH – DESERT HIDE-OUT

6914 East Continental Mountain, Cave Creek, AZ 85331   *602-488-1855*
Dennis & JoDean Loveless, Resident Owners   *FAX 602-488-1855*

LOCATION	From Cave Creek Road in the center of town go north on School House Road about a mile. Turn right (east) on Fleming Springs Road and travel .8 mile and turn right (south) on Echo Canyon (gravel road) travel about 100 yards and turn left (east) on Continental Mountain Road to first driveway on the left.
OPEN	All year
DESCRIPTION	1960 Frank Lloyd Wright student-designed home with a five acre horse ranch and traditional western ranch furnishings.
NO. OF ROOMS	Three rooms with private bathrooms. Pick the Ranch Master Room.
RATES	Year round rates for a single or a double with a private bathroom are $55 to $65. The bunk house is $25 per person and the entire B&B rents for $25 per person. Ask about minimum stay and cancellation.
CREDIT CARDS	No
BREAKFAST	Continental Plus is served in the dining room and includes fresh fruit and baked goods, cereals, yogurts, toast, juice, coffee and tea.
AMENITIES	Swimming pool, hot tub, fire ring, bunkhouse, saloon, horse boarding.
RESTRICTIONS	No smoking in house, patio okay. There are four resident dogs, unnumbered cats and at least 10 horses.

DEBRA ANN'S BED & BREAKFAST

6101 Victoria Drive, Cave Creek, AZ 85331   *602-488-2644*
Debra Ann & Gaines Du Vall, Resident Owners

LOCATION	Take I-17 north from Phoenix to the Carefree Highway exit. Turn right (east) and then 12 miles to Cave Creek Road. Turn left (north) and go 1.6 miles to Surrey Road. Turn right (east) to Victoria Drive, go up the mountain and back down the mountain to a dead end at the B&B.
OPEN	August 15 through May 31, closed during the summer and December 15 through January 14.
DESCRIPTION	A 1980 Territorial with Territorial furnishings.
NO. OF ROOMS	Two rooms with shared bathrooms. Pick the King Bedroom.
RATES	Year-round rates for a single or a double with a shared bathroom are $90 to $95 and the entire B&B rents for $170. There is a two night minimum stay and cancellation requires seven days notice with a $10 fee.
CREDIT CARDS	No
BREAKFAST	Continental Plus is self-serve in the family room and includes fresh fruit, bagels, sweet rolls, cold and hot cereals, milk, juice, coffee and tea.
AMENITIES	Fresh flowers in each room with a snack-filled welcome basket, robes, fireplace, wet bar, refrigerator and microwave in living area, TV/VCR.
RESTRICTIONS	No smoking, no pets, no children, one guest car per bedroom.

GOTLAND'S BLACK MOUNTAIN BED & BREAKFAST

38555 North Schoolhouse Road, Cave Creek, AZ 85331   *602-488-9636*
Jan & Al Gotland, Resident Owners   *FAX 602-488-9636*

LOCATION	Cave Creek is 28 miles north of Sky Harbor Airport in Phoenix. The B&B is .3 mile north of Cave Creek Road on Schoolhouse, the first house north of Desert Foothills Library.
OPEN	All year
DESCRIPTION	A 1950s Western guest ranch with private guest house accommodations.
NO. OF ROOMS	Four rooms with private bathrooms. Pick the main guest house.
RATES	Year-round rates for a single or a double with a private bathroom are $110 to $150. There is a two night minimum stay and cancellation requires seven days notice.
CREDIT CARDS	MasterCard, Visa
BREAKFAST	Continental Plus is served in the guestrooms and includes assorted Danish, muffins, cinnamon rolls, juice, fruit basket and snack basket.
AMENITIES	Robes, phone, cable TV, saloon, petting zoo, horse shoes, steak fries, horseback rides.
RESTRICTIONS	No smoking, no pets, children over 12 are welcome. The Greyhound is Elvis and there are all sorts of horses and goats.
KUDOS/COMMENTS	"Private guesthouse, very quiet and nice."

VERDE CABALLO RANCH B&B

41848 North Fleming Springs Road, Cave Creek, AZ 85331   602-488-0264
Jeff & Tami George, Resident Owners

LOCATION	Take Cave Creek Road into the "frontier town" and go north on School House Road. At the stop sign, turn right on Fleming Springs Road. The B&B is the first house on the left after the road turns to gravel.
OPEN	All year
DESCRIPTION	A 1974 ranch house with Southwestern furnishings; located on seven acres.
NO. OF ROOMS	One room with private bathroom and an additional room for guests of the same party.
RATES	Year-round rate for a single or a double with a private bathroom is $85 and $15 more per person to use the additional room. There is no minimum stay and cancellation requires seven days notice.
CREDIT CARDS	No
BREAKFAST	Continental Plus is served in the guestroom and includes basket of fruit, gourmet coffee, hot chocolate, tea, hot and cold cereal, fresh baked muffins and rolls, milk and assorted juices.
AMENITIES	TV/VCR, private patio, horse boarding, guest kitchenette.
RESTRICTIONS	No smoking, no pets. There are three resident dogs, Fresca, Jeta & Allie; two cats, Yoda and Blue, and 20 horses.

CHLORIDE

Twenty five miles north of Kingman and 50 miles south of Boulder Dam. A quiet, low key small town. Try a summer weekend with Friday night street dancing and free melodrama on the first and third Saturday evenings.

SHEPS BED & BREAKFAST

9819 2nd Street, Chloride, AZ 86431   520-565-3643
William L. McAdams, Resident Owner   FAX 520-565-4251
Spanish and some Arabic spoken

LOCATION	One block south of town center.
OPEN	All year
DESCRIPTION	A 1910 country Victorian with Victorian and Western furnishings. Listing on the National and State Historic Registers is pending.
NO. OF ROOMS	Two rooms with private bathrooms and two rooms share two bathrooms. William McAdams suggests #4 as his best room.
RATES	Year-round rate for a single or a double with private bathroom is $55 and a single or a double with a shared bathroom is $45. There is no minimum stay and cancellation requires 24 hours and a $10 fee.
CREDIT CARDS	MasterCard, Visa
BREAKFAST	Full breakfast is served in the restaurant next door and is cooked to order plus fresh daily breads, fresh fruit, fresh squeezed juice, rolls and coffee. Breakfast may also be served in bed on request.
AMENITIES	Solar heated "stock tank" under water tower, enclosed patio, horseback riding, bicycle rental and hiking trails nearby.
RESTRICTIONS	No smoking, no pets, no children. Resident dog.
REVIEWED	Just opening in early 1995.
MEMBER	Professional Association of Innkeepers International

CLARKDALE

The "Old Town" two miles northwest of Cottonwood via Highway 89A and Highway 279. Fish the Verde River in Dead Horse State Park.

FLYING EAGLE COUNTRY BED & BREAKFAST

2700 Windmill Lane, Clarkdale, AZ 86324   520-634-0663
Cristus & Inger Bellamy, Resident Owner

KUDOS/COMMENTS   "Lovely setting, charming hostess, the accommodations are great and so is breakfast"

CLIFTON

In the extreme eastern part of Arizona this mining town is the home to one of the largest copper mines in the country and the Geronimo Festival in early July.

THE POTTER RANCH BED & BREAKFAST

PO Box 843, Clifton, AZ 85533   520-865-4847
June Palmer, Resident Owner

CORNVILLE

In the Verde Valley, 24 miles southwest of Sedona and five miles southeast of Cottonwood via US 17 & Highway 89. Close to Montezuma Castle National Monument.

COUNTRY ELEGANCE
BED & BREAKFAST

PO Box 564, Cornville, AZ 86325   520-634-4470
Carl & Cindy Miller, Resident Owners

PUMPKINSHELL RANCH
BED & BREAKFAST

11005 East Johnson Road, Cornville, AZ 86325   520-634-4797
Blair & Eleanor Paulsen, Resident Owners

DOUGLAS

Located on the Mexican border 117 miles southeast of Tucson via I-10 and Highway 80. Originally an annual round-up site for cattle ranchers. Visit the Slaughter Ranch/San Bernardino National Wildlife Refuge and in May don't miss the Great American Bed Race or the D.A.R.C. Cake Auction.

FAMILY CREST BED & BREAKFAST

910 East Avenue, Douglas, AZ 85608   520-364-3998
Inis R. Tashiro, Resident Owner

LOCATION	In Douglas, turn left at the light past the Gadson Hotel, second street is East Avenue, middle house.
OPEN	All year
DESCRIPTION	A two-story 1904-1914 red brick home with Oriental and antique furnishings.
NO. OF ROOMS	Three rooms with private bathrooms and three rooms share two bathrooms. Pick the largest bedroom.
RATES	Year-round rates for a single or a double with a private bathroom are $45 to $65. There is no minimum stay and no cancellation policy.
CREDIT CARDS	MasterCard, Visa
BREAKFAST	Continental breakfast is served in the dining room and includes fruit, coffee cake, muffins, juice, coffee, tea.
AMENITIES	Flowers or fruit, candies.
RESTRICTIONS	No smoking, no pets, no children, The German Shepherd is Tara and the bird is Sammy.

DRAGOON

In the heart of the Dragoon Mountains, named for the 3rd U.S. Cavalry Dragoons, 60 miles southeast of Tucson and 30 miles southwest of Willcox via I-10. Check out the archaeological exhibits and art gallery at the Amerind Foundation Museum and visit Cochise Stronghold Canyon 10 miles from town.

KELLY'S WHISTLESTOP BED & BREAKFAST

107 Perry Road, Dragoon, AZ 85609   520-586-7515
Jim & Katy Kelly, Resident Owners

LOCATION	From exit 318 on I-10 travel east on Dragoon Road 3.2 miles to Perry Road and bear right to the first drive on the right.
OPEN	All year
DESCRIPTION	1981 modern Southwest with guesthouse on four acres with locally acquired antique southwestern furnishings.
NO. OF ROOMS	Two bedrooms in the guesthouse share one bathroom. Pick the south bedroom.
RATES	Year-round rates are $45 to $55 for a single or a double and $95 to $105 for the entire guesthouse. There is no minimum stay and cancellation requires three days notice.
CREDIT CARDS	No
BREAKFAST	Full breakfast is served in the dining room and includes omelette, breakfast burrito, several different French toasts, Irish oat meal, scones, homemade muffins, sourdough pancakes.
AMENITIES	Hot tub on the main house patio, guesthouse is stocked with fresh ground coffee, teas, spiced cider or hot chocolate. Let the innkeepers know if you are celebrating an anniversary.
RESTRICTIONS	No smoking, well-behaved pets with responsible owners can be accommodated with prior notice, children over 12 are welcome. There are two resident dogs, Grace and Li'l Fox, two cats called Tarzan and Nut and a Tennessee Walker called Sonny...This was the most neatly printed survey we received from an Arizona B&B, thank you...TI
REVIEWED	*Fodor's - The Southwest*

*E*AGAR

Located near the Apache Sitgreaves National Forest and the Casa Malapais Ruins, Eagar is neat little ranching and lumber industry town near the mountain, good fishing and hiking.

COYOTE CREEK CATTLE COMPANY

PO Box 277, Eagar, AZ 85925   *520-333-5521*
Michael & Jeanne Udall, Resident Owners

PAISLEY CORNERS B&B

287 North Main, Eagar, AZ 85925   *520-333-4665*
Sheryl & Cletus Tisdale, Resident Owners

FLAGSTAFF

In north central alpine country, at the foot of lofty San Francisco Peaks, via I-40 & I-17, this is the home to Northern Arizona University. Don't miss the Sinagua cliff dwellings in Walnut Canyon National Monument, the celestial bodies at Lowell Observatory, and astrogeology at the U.S. Geological Survey. There's good skiing in the Fairfield Snow Bowl and Flagstaff Nordic Center, and summer is filled with major art Festivals. And, yes, Flagstaff is named for a flagpole.

ARIZONA MOUNTAIN INN

685 Lake Mary Road, Flagstaff, AZ 86001   520-774-8959
Ray & Pauline Wanek, Resident Owners

LOCATION	Two miles from downtown. One mile on Lake Mary Road off Highway 89 and I-17.
OPEN	All Year
DESCRIPTION	1979 two-story Tudor manor with Old English and Southwestern country furnishings plus 16 cottages and chalets on 13 acres.
NO. OF ROOMS	Three rooms with private bathrooms and four rooms share one bathroom. Ray recommends the honeymoon suite.
RATES	Year-round rate for a single or a double with a private bathroom is $100 and a single or a double with a shared bathroom is $70. There is no minimum stay although a rate card says there is a minimum weekend stay … ask.
CREDIT CARDS	Discover, MasterCard, Visa
BREAKFAST	Continental breakfast is served in the dining room and includes fresh fruit, assorted cereals and juices, toast and hot sweet rolls, coffee and tea. (Not included for cottages and chalets.)
AMENITIES	Fireplaces, complimentary refreshments, volleyball court, horseshoes.
RESTRICTIONS	No smoking, no pets, no children in the inn, but all are allowed in the cottages and chalets.
REVIEWED	*Non-Smokers Guide to B&Bs, Official Bed & Breakfast Guide.*
KUDOS/COMMENTS	"Very homey and the hosts are very friendly, located in the pines."

BIRCH TREE INN B&B

824 West Birch Avenue, Flagstaff, AZ 86001
Sandy & Ed Znetko and
Donna & Rodger Pettinger, Resident Owners

520-774-1042
800-645-5811
FAX 520-774-4209

LOCATION	Exit 195B from Highway 40, take Milton four miles to Highway 180 (following signs directing to Grand Canyon). Turn left, go two streets to Birch Avenue; turn left. Proceed six blocks to inn.
OPEN	All year
DESCRIPTION	A 1917 Craftsman farmhouse bungalow with country furnishings, Corinthian columns and sidewrap porch.
NO. OF ROOMS	Three rooms with private bathrooms and two rooms share one bathroom. Sandy suggests the Southwest Room as her best.
RATES	Year-round rates for a single or a double with a private bathroom are $65 to $80 and $55 to $60 for a single or a double with a shared bathroom. The entire B&B rents for $340. There is no minimum stay and cancellation requires 72 hours notice and a $10 cancellation fee.
CREDIT CARDS	Amex, MasterCard, Visa
BREAKFAST	Full breakfast is served in the dining room and includes egg casserole with meat, fresh baked breads, fruit, coffee, tea or waffles, pancakes and homemade syrups.
AMENITIES	Game room with pool table, fireplace and TV in common area. Afternoon refreshments served outside in the summer. Special gifts for celebrants and the innkeepers can accommodate small weddings and receptions, especially in the summer months.
RESTRICTIONS	No smoking, no pets and children over 10 are welcome. The resident Cocker Spaniel is called Daisy.
REVIEWED	*Journey to the High Southwest, Recommended Country Inns of the Southwest, Fodor's - The Southwest, Hidden Southwest, Ultimate Southwest, Arizona Handbook*
MEMBER	Professional Association of Innkeepers International, Arizona Association of Bed & Breakfast Innkeepers, Northern Arizona Innkeepers Association
AWARDS	Commendation for Historic Preservation 1990 from the Flagstaff City Council.

COMFICOTTAGES OF FLAGSTAFF

1612 North Aztec, Flagstaff, AZ 86001   *520-774-0731*
Pat & Ed Wiebe, Resident Owners

LOCATION	Five cottages at various locations in downtown historic district on Beaver, Birch and Columbus Streets.
OPEN	All year
DESCRIPTION	Four 1920s restored cottages with English country furnishings and one cottage with Southwestern furnishings.
NO. OF ROOMS	All the cottages have a bathroom, living room, and kitchen, there is 1 one-bedroom cottage, 3 two-bedroom cottages and 1 three-bedroom cottage. "The cottage at 710 Birch is the nicest."
RATES	Year-round rates for a single or a double with a private bathroom range from $65 to $185, and $60 for a single or a double with a shared bathroom. There is a two night minimum on the weekends and a cancellation policy.
CREDIT CARDS	MasterCard, Visa
BREAKFAST	Full breakfast includes bacon, eggs, juice, milk, bread, baskets of muffins and fresh fruit stocked in the refrigerator for the guest's preparation.
AMENITIES	Fully equipped cottages, cable TV and telephones in rooms, fully equipped kitchens, complimentary bikes, sleds, picnic table, BBQ and tennis racquets.
RESTRICTIONS	No smoking except outside. Inquire about pets, all children are welcome.
REVIEWED	*Bed & Breakfast & Country Inns, From Sea to Shining Sea.*
MEMBER	Professional Association of Innkeepers International

DIERKER HOUSE

423 West Cherry, Flagstaff, AZ 86001
Dorothea Dierker, Resident Owner

520-774-3249

LOCATION	In Historic District, five blocks west of downtown.
OPEN	All year
DESCRIPTION	1914 late Victorian with antique furnishings. Listed on National and State Historic Registers.
NO. OF ROOMS	Three rooms with shared bathrooms. Pick Germany as the best room.
RATES	Year-round rates for a single or a double with a shared bathroom are $50. There is two day minimum stay on the weekends and there is a cancellation policy.
CREDIT CARDS	No
BREAKFAST	Full breakfast is served at 8:00 a.m. in dining room. (Continental plus, earlier or later, served in guest kitchen). The full breakfast includes eggs, meat, potatoes, toast, muffins, juice, fruit and coffees.
AMENITIES	Complimentary wine, coffee, tea, crackers & cookies in guest kitchen.
RESTRICTIONS	No smoking, no pets, children over 12 are welcome. The resident Shi-Tzus are Sadie and Sallie and the eight Canaries are named after singers... Any of them named Jimmy Buffet? Should be...TI
REVIEWED	*Bed & Breakfast U.S.A.*

EAST CHERRY INN BED & BREAKFAST

427 East Cherry Avenue, Flagstaff, AZ 86001 520-774-1153
Paula Martini & Jim Cross, Resident Owners
Some Spanish spoken

LOCATION	From the Flagstaff train station go north three blocks to Cherry Avenue, turn right and go 4 1/2 blocks up a steep hill.
OPEN	All year (suite).
DESCRIPTION	A 1964 two-story Ranch with Southwestern, antique and modern furnishings.
NO. OF ROOMS	One suite with private bathroom, one room shares one bathroom. Pick the Southwestern Suite.
RATES	Year-round rates for a single or a double with a private bathroom are $80 to $120, a single or a double with a shared bathroom is $65. There is a two night minimum on the suite on weekends and holidays. Cancellation requires seven days notice with a $15 fee.
CREDIT CARDS	No
BREAKFAST	Continental Plus is served in the dining room and includes fresh baked pastries, milk, orange juice, fresh ground coffee, tea, hot chocolate, seasonal fruit, cereal and yogurt.
AMENITIES	The suite has a woodburning stove, piano, phone, TV, sunroom and full kitchen, TV/VCR in living room, guidebooks and deck.
RESTRICTIONS	No smoking, no pets, children over eight welcome in the suite. The inn caters to the chemically and environmentally sensitive.

INN AT 410 BED & BREAKFAST

410 North Leroux Street, Flagstaff, AZ 86001   520-774-0088
Howard & Sally Krueger, Resident Owners   800-774-2008

LOCATION	From I-40 take exit 195B north onto Milton. Follow Milton under railroad overpass and curve to the right. Turn left at the first stoplight (Humphreys). At Dale turn right. Turn left on Leroux, then turn right into parking lot.
OPEN	All year
DESCRIPTION	1907 modified Craftsman with 1944 and 1990 additions and eclectic furnishings.
NO. OF ROOMS	Eight rooms with private bathrooms. Pick the Tea Room.
RATES	Year-round rates for a single or a double with a private bathroom are $90 to $135. There is a two night minimum stay from May 1 through October 31 and three days on some holidays. Cancellation requires seven days notice.
CREDIT CARDS	Amex, MasterCard, Visa
BREAKFAST	Full breakfast is served in the dining room includes juice, fruit cup, fresh baked muffins or scones, gourmet entree that is low fat and low cholesterol when possible, and hot beverage.
AMENITIES	Afternoon cookies, and seasonal beverage, fireplace in the living room, patio, gazebo. Mini-fridges and coffeemakers in each room, some rooms have fireplaces or whirlpool tubs, one room is wheelchair accessible, small meeting facilities.
RESTRICTIONS	No smoking, no pets. Lucy is the resident Schnauzer but she, "is not part of the inn experience."
REVIEWED	*Fodor's - The Southwest, Bed & Breakfast Guide Southwest, Best Places to Stay in the Southwest, Recommended Country Inns: The Southwest, Weekends for Two in the Southwest, America's Wonderful Little Hotels & Inns*
MEMBER	Professional Association of Innkeepers International, Arizona Association of Bed & Breakfast Inns, American Bed & Breakfast Association
RATED	AAA 2 Diamonds, ABBA 2 Crowns
AWARDS	Best Place for a Weekend Getaway in Flagstaff, *The Arizona Republic*, 1992.

PINEY WOODS LODGE

2800 West Hogan Drive #6, Flagstaff, AZ 86001   520-774-8859
Dan & Jill White, Resident Owners

SAN FRANCISCO STREET BED & BREAKFAST

622 North San Francisco Street, Flagstaff, AZ 86001   520-779-2257
Freda & Marvin Van Houten, Resident Owners

LOCATION	Six blocks north of Route 66.
OPEN	All year
DESCRIPTION	A 1937 two-story English country host home with some antiques and country eclectic furnishings.
NO. OF ROOMS	Three rooms with shared bathrooms. The best is the Rose Room.
RATES	Year-round rates for a single or a double with a shared bathroom are $45 to $60. There is a two-day minimum stay on the weekends and a cancellation policy.
CREDIT CARDS	No
BREAKFAST	Full breakfast served in the dining room with an emphasis on health foods, i.e., whole grains, fresh fruit, vegetarian omelettes.
AMENITIES	Fireplace in the living room and parlor, pool table, private sitting and reading room and phone is available.
RESTRICTIONS	No smoking, no pets, children over 12 are welcome.
REVIEWED	*Fodor's - The Southwest*

STARLIT FARM BED & BREAKFAST

8455 Koch Field Road, Flagstaff, AZ 86004   520-526-1173
Tobie & Bernie Trejo, Resident Owners   800-484-7389—code 5759

FLORENCE

Located 50 miles southeast of Phoenix at the intersection of Highways 89 and 287.

INN AT RANCHO SONORA

9198 North Highway 79, Florence, AZ 85232   520-868-8000
Linda & Brent Freeman, Resident Owners   800-205-6817
Spanish spoken

LOCATION	Five and a half miles south of Florence on the west side of Highway 79, one quarter mile north of the intersection of Highway 79 and Cactus Forest Road.
OPEN	All year
DESCRIPTION	A 1930s restored adobe Territorial hacienda and guesthouse with fountain and Spanish courtyard, furnished with Southwestern antiques and Victorian.
NO. OF ROOMS	Six rooms with private bathrooms. Dolores is best room in the house.
RATES	High season, October through April, rates for a single or a double with a private bathroom are $49 to $59 and the guesthouse is $85. Off season, May through September, rates for a single or a double are $40 to $49 and $50 for the guesthouse. There is no minimum stay and innkeepers require 48 hours notice for cancellation.
CREDIT CARDS	Amex, Discover, MasterCard, Visa
BREAKFAST	Continental breakfast is served in the kitchenette room and includes several kinds of pastries, homebaked breads, fresh fruit, nuts and cereals, juices, coffee, tea, chocolate and espresso. Other meals are available for special group occasions by reservations.
AMENITIES	Patio and hot tub, pool, TV in all rooms, phone available, meeting facilities for up to 20; and 20 hookups and day camping areas removed from the B&B but part of the facility.
RESTRICTIONS	Smoking in certain areas, small pets are okay. The resident dog is Max and the cat is Renee.
REVIEWED	*Recommended Country Inn Southwest*

FOUNTAIN HILLS
(PHOENIX)

The world's highest fountain shoots 560 feet into the air in this community 18 miles northeast of Scottsdale, via Highway 87 & Shea Boulevard. Check out the world's biggest cats at the Out of Africa Wildlife Park.

BEDLAM BED & BREAKFAST

15225 Wiley Drive, Fountain Hills, AZ 85268   602-837-9695
Tom & Pam Carlson, Resident Owners

LOCATION	5 miles northeast of Scottsdale, via Highway 87 or Shea Boulevard. Take Fountain HIlls Boulevard to El Pueblo to Wiley Drive.
OPEN	All Year
DESCRIPTION	1989 Southwestern with antique & Southwestern furnishings
NO. OF ROOMS	Guesthouse with private bath
RATES	Inquire. Varies with seasons.
CREDIT CARDS	No
BREAKFAST	Full, Continental Plus or continental, served in dining room, guesthouse or back porch.
AMENITIES	Swimming pool, hot tub, TV/radio in rooms, phone in room by request; babysitting available.
RESTRICTIONS	No smoking. Resident dog & pond fish.

EAGLE HOUSE BED & BREAKFAST

10621 Eagle Lane, Fountain Hills, AZ 85268   602-837-7072
Steven Werro, Resident Owner

FOUNTAIN HILLS BED & BREAKFAST

16240 Kingstreet Boulevard, Fountain Hills, AZ 85268   602-837-8909
Randy & Jane Johnston, Resident Owners   800-484-9746 ext. 4646

LOCATION	From Sky Harbor Airport exit 44 to McDowell, east on McDowell to Highway 87, turn left 10 miles to Shea Boulevard, turn left, go .5 mile to Saguaro Boulevard and turn right. Continue two miles to Kingstreet and turn left, at the top of the hill turn right into driveway.
OPEN	November 1 to May 1
DESCRIPTION	A 1972 California ranch with antique and southwestern furnishings.
NO. OF ROOMS	One room with private bathroom and two rooms share one bathroom.
RATES	Seasonal rates for a single or a double with a private bathroom are $65, and $55 for a single or a double with a shared bathroom. There in no minimum stay and cancellation requires seven days notice.
CREDIT CARDS	No
BREAKFAST	Full breakfast is served in the dining room and includes fruit, juice, coffee, breads, eggs, sausage or bacon, fancy dishes and silver service.
AMENITIES	Outdoor spa on deck, TV, telephone, alarm clocks, robes in each room, two rooms have large decks with views, pond and wildlife.
RESTRICTIONS	Smoking on porch or deck only, no pets, children over seven are welcome. Scooter is the dog and about 20 Gambell's Quail live in the yard.

SYCAMORE CANYON BED & BREAKFAST

15807 Sycamore Drive, Fountain Hills, AZ 85268   602-837-1175
Nan & Mark Lesnick, Resident Owners

GLOBE

Active copper mining town 88 miles west of Phoenix via Highway 60, trading center for San Carlos Apache Indian Reservation. Check out Cobre Valley Center for the Arts, Besh-ba-Gowah Indian Ruins, Copper Dust Stampede Days in April, Apache Days in October.

CEDAR HILL BED & BREAKFAST

175 East Cedar, Globe, AZ 85501   520-425-7530
Helen Gross, Resident Owner

LOCATION	Half a block from the stop light at Broad and Cedar in downtown Globe.
OPEN	All year
DESCRIPTION	A 1907 two-story lumber baron's home with country furnishings.
NO. OF ROOMS	Two rooms with shared bathrooms. Pick the paneled back porch as the best room in the house.
RATES	Year-round rates for a single or a double with a shared bathroom are $50. There is no minimum stay and no reservation or cancellation policy.
CREDIT CARDS	No
BREAKFAST	Full breakfast is served in the dining room and includes fruit, juice, muffins, toast, eggs any style, ham or bacon, coffee and tea.
RESTRICTIONS	Smoking on the porch or patio only, children are welcome. The resident friendly Collie is Cassie.
REVIEWED	*Bed & Breakfast Guide*

NOFTSGER HILL INN

425 North Street, Globe, AZ 85501   520-425-2260
Frank & Pam Hulme, Resident Owners

KUDOS/COMMENTS	"A remodeled elementary school that gives an impression of unlimited space and attention to detail."

PINAL MOUNTAIN BED & BREAKFAST

360 Jess Hayes Road, Globe, AZ 85502   520-425-2562
Carol & Peter DeNinno, Resident Owners   FAX 520-425-0113

LOCATION	One miles south of town, next to Besh-ba-Gowah archaeological ruins.
OPEN	All year
DESCRIPTION	Guesthouse with Southwestern furnishings on a working horse farm.
NO. OF ROOMS	Two rooms with private bathrooms.
RATES	Year-round rates for a single or a double with a private bathroom are $60 to $75 and the entire guesthouse rents for $120 to $150. There is no minimum stay and the innkeepers require 10 days notice for cancellation.
CREDIT CARDS	No
BREAKFAST	Continental Plus is served in the common area of the guesthouse and includes fresh fruit, assorted hot and cold beverages, assorted hot and cold cereals, fresh eggs, hot muffins and bagels.
AMENITIES	TV/VCR, radio and phone located in the guesthouse common area in addition to a fully equipped kitchen with a microwave. The guesthouse is handicapped accessible. Horse corrals rent for $5 per night.
RESTRICTIONS	No smoking, no pets. There are 25 resident Paso Fino horses that are a "special breed of gaited horses that don't trot." Cowlamity Jane is the resident Hereford, Roosevelt is the dog, Barkley & Tracey are the cats, Hansel & Gretel are the geese and Chloe & Pepe are the pygmy goats.

GOODYEAR
(PHOENIX)

A small community eight miles west of Phoenix via I-10. The Estrella Mountain Regional Park, with 18,600 acres of rugged desert terrain and an 18-hole golf course is a surprise.

INDIAN SPRINGS RANCH
BED & BREAKFAST

13132 West Beverly Road, Goodyear, AZ 85338   *602-932-2076*
Frank & Elaine Billingsley, Resident Owners
Spanish and French spoken

LOCATION	I-10 exit 131 south on 115th Avenue 5.5 miles to Phoenix International Raceway. The highway bends west and becomes Indian Springs Road. Go two miles to 133rd Avenue and turn south one block to Beverly Road then turn east to first house on the north side.
OPEN	October 1 to April 15.
DESCRIPTION	1974 two-story Spanish Hacienda and guest house with Spanish/Mexican furnishings.
NO. OF ROOMS	Four rooms with private bathrooms and two rooms share one bathroom. Frank says the Frontier Room is his best.
RATES	Seasonal rates for a single or a double with a private bathroom are $55 to $75, and $55 for a single or a double with a shared bathroom. The guest house is $65 for two and $85 for four. There is no minimum stay and the cancellation policy, "none, please call as soon as possible." ...That's a seriously guest oriented policy that shows true hospitality...One thumb up Frank!...TI
CREDIT CARDS	No
BREAKFAST	Continental Plus, served in dining room, patio or guestroom and includes coffee, juice, tea, muffins, toast, fruit, cereal, milk and Danish.
AMENITIES	Swimming pool, telephone only in main house, golf course and 18,000 acre Estrella Park adjacent with horse back riding, hiking and climbing. Seven gold courses within 12 miles, bird watching.
RESTRICTIONS	Smoking only on patios next to rooms, no pets. The resident German Shepherd is a friendly Lady.

GREER

A pristine recreation area in the high White Mountains, named for Mormon pioneer Americus Vespucius Greer, 16 miles west of Springerville and Eagar via Highway 260 & 373. Skiing at Sunrise Ski Area, and cross-country trails everywhere else. Great fishing in Greer lakes, and hiking access to Mount Baldy Wilderness. WARNING: The cancellation policies in Greer are absurd.

GREER LODGE BED & BREAKFAST

PO Box 244, Greer, AZ 85927   520-735-7515
Gerald Scott, Manager

RED SETTER INN

8 Main Street, Greer, AZ 85927   520-735-7441
Jim Sankey, Resident Owner

LOCATION	Highway 373 turns into Main Street in Greer.
OPEN	All year
DESCRIPTION	A 1995 log lodge with "lodge style" furnishings and antiques; located on the Little Colorado River.
NO. OF ROOMS	Eight rooms with private bathrooms.
RATES	Year-round rates for a single or a double with a private bathroom are $105 to $145. There is a two night minimum stay on the weekends and three nights on holiday weekends, cancellation requires 30 days notice.
CREDIT CARDS	Amex, MasterCard, Visa
BREAKFAST	Full breakfast is served in the dining room and includes cereals, juice, coffee, "full cooked breakfast of the day."
AMENITIES	Jacuzzi tubs, private fireplaces, video library, bird watching, fishing, hiking, X-C skiing, small meeting facility and limited wheelchair access.
RESTRICTIONS	No smoking, no pets, children over 16 are welcome. The mixed Lab is called Dafton.

Snowy Mountain Inn

Route 373, Greer, AZ 85927   520-735-7567
Cynthia & Steve Matheson, Resident Owners   FAX 520-735-7705

LOCATION	From Highway 260 go south on Highway 373 1.4 miles, inn is on the left.
OPEN	All year
DESCRIPTION	A 1958 two-story country inn and cabins, all wood on walls, floors and ceilings.
NO. OF ROOMS	Four rooms with private bathrooms. Pick the suite.
RATES	Year-round rates for a single or a double with a private bathroom are $69 to $75, the suite is $85 and cabins are $110. There is a minimum stay on the weekends and no refund if the room is not rebooked.
CREDIT CARDS	No
BREAKFAST	Continental breakfast is served in the dining room and includes fresh fruit, juice, coffee, tea, breads and muffins. Dinner and special meals with notice.
AMENITIES	Spa, robes, restaurant and bar, meeting facilities, pond.
RESTRICTIONS	No smoking, no pets in lodge, the horses are called Raven and Carlie.

WHITE MOUNTAIN LODGE

140 Main Street, Greer, AZ 85927   520-735-7568
Charles & Mary Bast, Resident Owners   FAX 520-735-7498
Spanish spoken

LOCATION	Downtown Greer
OPEN	All year
DESCRIPTION	1892 restored (1994) two-story farmhouse and cabins with Southwestern and country furnishings.
NO. OF ROOMS	Seven rooms with private bathrooms. Pick #2.
RATES	Year-round rates for a single or a double with a private bathroom are $60 to $70 and the cabins are $60 to $95. There is a two day minimum stay on weekends and three days on holidays. A 50% deposit is returned only if the room is rented for the entire length of the reservation.
CREDIT CARDS	No
BREAKFAST	Full breakfast is served in the dining room and includes pancakes, sausage, bacon, ham, coffeecake, juice, casserole, homemade banana bread, toast, muffins, fresh fruit, eggs benedict.
AMENITIES	Hot drinks and homemade treats in the late afternoon and early evening, guest refrigerator, TV and FAX available.
RESTRICTIONS	No smoking in bedrooms, only in designated areas.
REVIEWED	*Arizona Traveler's Handbook, Country Inns of Arizona, New Mexico & Texas, Fodor's - The Southwest*

HEREFORD

Adjacent to the Nature Conservancy's Mile Hi/Ramsey Canyon Preserve, home to more than 100 species of birds. Between Sierra Vista and Bisbee via Highway 92.

RAMSEY CANYON INN

31 Ramsey Canyon Road, Hereford, AZ 85615   520-378-3010
Shirlene DeSantis, Resident Owner

LOCATION	From Sierra Vista take Highway 92 south to Ramsey Canyon Road (about 6.5 miles), then turn right and go 3.5 miles to the B&B on the right.
OPEN	All year.
DESCRIPTION	1960-1987 contemporary country inn with antique and country furnishings.
NO. OF ROOMS	Six rooms with private bathrooms, plus two housekeeping cottages. Pick room #3 says Shirlene.
RATES	Year-round rates for a single or a double with a private bathroom are $90 to $105 and the cottages are $95 to $115. There is a two day minimum stay in the cottages and on holidays in the B&B. Cancellation requires 14 days notice.
CREDIT CARDS	No
BREAKFAST	Full gourmet breakfast served in the dining room is different every day and might be something like blue corn pancakes, eggs olé, Dutch pancakes or eggs Italiano. Homemade pies (Shirlene has over 100 blue ribbons for her pies) are served in the afternoons.
AMENITIES	Ramsey Canyon is the "hummingbird capital of the world with 15 species recorded", hiking trails, no TV, no telephones…blue ribbon pies, hummers, and no TV and phone, sounds perfect…TI
RESTRICTIONS	Smoking restricted to the patio, no pets, children welcome in the cottages. The resident Yorkie is Megan.
REVIEWED	*Arizona Handbook*
KUDOS/COMMENTS	"Great B&B in the mountains south of Tucson, wildlife, especially birds."

JEROME

The picturesque historic copper mining town clings to the sides of Cleopatra Hill above the Verde Valley. Now restored as an art center with shops, museums and galleries. The historic Home Tour in May and fall Music Festival are major events. From Cottonwood go eight miles west via Highway 89A.

THE COTTAGE INN

747 East Avenue, Jerome, AZ 86331   520-634-0701
Al Palmieri and J. Armstrong, Resident Owners

LOCATION	A half mile from the middle of town, next street after the Methodist Church, third house on the right.
OPEN	All year
DESCRIPTION	1904 Victorian with antique furnishings. On the National Historic Register.
NO. OF ROOMS	Two rooms share two bathrooms.
RATES	Year-round rate for a single or double is $60. There is no minimum stay and cancellation requires 24 hours notice.
CREDIT CARDS	Amex, Diners Club, Discover, MasterCard, Visa
BREAKFAST	Full breakfast served in the dining room.
AMENITIES	Private patio and porch with potted plants and flowers.
RESTRICTIONS	None. The two dogs are Pepper and Puddy and the cat is Sugar.

GHOST CITY INN

541 Main Street, Jerome, AZ 86331   520-634-4678
Bob & Judy Jackson, Managers   FAX 520-634-4678

LOCATION	Greater downtown Jerome
OPEN	All year
DESCRIPTION	An 1898 restored two-story home with antique furnishings; listed on the State Historic Register.
NO. OF ROOMS	Six rooms share three bathrooms. Judy suggests a room called Hearts & Flowers.
RATES	Year-round rates for a single or a double with a shared bathroom are $65 to $85. There is no minimum stay and cancellation requires seven days notice.
CREDIT CARDS	Amex, Discover, MasterCard, Visa
BREAKFAST	Full breakfast served in the dining room.
AMENITIES	Afternoon tea and cookies, two common guest areas, TV, robes, phones and FAX.
RESTRICTIONS	No smoking, no pets and children over 10 are welcome. The resident Goldie is Chuck.
MEMBER	Arizona Association of Bed & Breakfast Inns

HILLSIDE HOUSE

687 Main, Jerome, AZ 86331   520-634-5667
Faith Matheus, Innkeeper
Adequate German spoken.

LOCATION	One half mile from uptown Jerome.
OPEN	All year
DESCRIPTION	A 1904 mining residence with eclectic furnishings that is listed on both the National and the State Historic Registers.
NO. OF ROOMS	Two room suite with private entrance.
RATES	Year-round rate for a single or a double with a private bathroom is $65. There is no minimum stay and the innkeeper requires a 50% deposit.
CREDIT CARDS	MasterCard, Visa
BREAKFAST	Continental breakfast is stocked in the refrigerator and includes fresh fruit, juices, hot and cold cereals, homemade fruit bread, cheeses, yogurt, milk, coffee and tea.
AMENITIES	Complimentary bottle of wine in the refrigerator, telephone, air conditioning, table games, microwave.
RESTRICTIONS	No pets, smoking on the patio only and children over seven are welcome. The resident longhaired cats are Charlotte and Gertie who are the official greeters, but "they do not go into the B&B area unless invited."
REVIEWED	*Fodor's Arizona*

THE SURGEON'S HOUSE

101 Hill Street, Jerome, AZ 86331   520-639-1452
Andrea Prince, Resident Owner   800-639-1452
Spanish and "minimal" French spoken.

LOCATION	Right on Main Street (Highway 89A) at T-intersection, proceed one block and continue as highway curves up and to the left. Follow for about two blocks, driveway is on the right across from the Jerome Palace.
OPEN	All year
DESCRIPTION	A 1916 two-story stucco European with eclectic, casual furnishings; listed on the National and State Historic Registers.
NO. OF ROOMS	Two rooms with private bathrooms and two rooms share one bathroom.
RATES	Year-round rates for a single or a double with a private bathroom are $65 to $85, suites are $100 and the entire B&B rents for $320. There is no minimum stay and cancellation requires "common sense, call with a reasonable problem in advance."...A+ Andrea...TI
CREDIT CARDS	No
BREAKFAST	Full breakfast is served in the dining room or outside patio and includes soup, juice, fresh fruit, baguette, muffin, cheeses, eggs, potatoes, smoked salmon, homemade mustard, yogurt and coffee.
AMENITIES	Flowers, hors d'oeuvres, robes, TV, phone, hot tub, in-house massage, complimentary beverages, midnight snack, picnics on request.
RESTRICTIONS	No smoking, pets allowed "within reason and with prior notice and well behaved children are welcome." The resident Labs are Katie and Max, and the two lovebirds are Gomez and Mitchell.
REVIEWED	Given how hard she worked on our survey, we think this might be a great inn, at the least a great innkeeper...TI

WHEELER'S BED & BREAKFAST

120 Juarez Street, Jerome, AZ 86331   520-634-3270
Jack & Anna Wheeler, Resident Owners

KINGMAN

The gateway to Lake Mead National Recreation Area. Kingman is 140 miles west of Flagstaff on I-40.

PINE LAKE INN

6902 Ponderosa, Kingman, AZ 86401   *520-757-9754*
Margaret & Marvin Moerbeck, Resident Owners
Italian spoken

LOCATION	In the Hualapai Mountains 14 miles out of Kingman. From I-40 at Kingman, take the Stockton Hill Road exit.
OPEN	All year
DESCRIPTION	A 1993 two-story contemporary with antique and contemporary furnishings; located on the shore of Pine Lake.
NO. OF ROOMS	Six rooms with private bathrooms.
RATES	Year-round rates for a single or a double with private bathroom are $95. There is no minimum stay and ask about a cancellation policy.
CREDIT CARDS	MasterCard
BREAKFAST	Full breakfast is served in the dining room and includes ham and bacon, eggs, fruit, juice, homemade bread and sweet rolls.
AMENITIES	Each room has a patio, feather beds and down comforters.
RESTRICTIONS	No smoking, no pets, no children. The resident cat is, "Kind and gentle."

LAKESIDE
(PINETOP)

Major summer and winter recreation area on the northeast edge of the White Mountain Apache Reservation. The twin towns of Lakeside and Pinetop lie near the edge of the Mogollon Rim. Winterfest at Sunrise Ski Area, and the White Mountain Native American Arts Festival and Indian Market in July are major events. From Holbrook, 57 miles south via Highway 77 and 73, and 10 miles southeast of Show Low off scenic US 60.

BARTRAM'S BED & BREAKFAST

Route 1, Box 1014, Lakeside, AZ 85929   520-367-1408
Petie & Ray Bartram, Resident Owners   800-257-0211

LOCATION	Take Highway 260 out of Show Low to Pinetop and Lakeside and go right at the intersection of Highway 260 and Woodland Road. Go one mile to stop sign, turn right to the dead end. The inn is the last house on the right.
OPEN	All year
DESCRIPTION	1940s ranch style with country furnishings.
NO. OF ROOMS	Three rooms with private bathrooms.
RATES	Year-round rates for a single or a double with a private bathroom are $60. The suite rents for $70 with a $20 charge for each bed occupied. There is a two-day minimum stay on the holidays and the innkeepers request one day deposit and cancellation requires 14 days notice prior to arrival for a full refund.
CREDIT CARDS	No
BREAKFAST	Full seven-course breakfast served family style in the dining room. Special meals available.
AMENITIES	Fresh flowers and candy in all guest rooms, hand decorated towels in the bathrooms and blow dryers and curling irons. Afternoon beverages and snacks. Living room with TV and games. The house is heated by a fireplace made of petrified wood.
RESTRICTIONS	No smoking. All children welcome and only female dogs allowed. The resident dogs are YumYum, Shammy and Wolfgang; the well-trained Pot Belly pigs are Farnsworth and Piggy Sue and parrot is Nugget.
REVIEWED	*Recommended Country Inns - The Southwest, Wake-Up and Smell the Coffee, Arizona Highway Cookbook.*
RATED	AAA 3 Diamonds
KUDOS/COMMENTS	"Comfortable rooms, good place to hike and great Collie who likes to hike with guests. Very friendly hosts."…"A classic B&B in the country with three rooms and its own resident pet pigs (2) !"

BILLINGS' COUNTRY RETREAT

63 East Turkey Track, Pinetop, AZ 85935   *520 367-1709*
Alice & Dave Billings, Resident Owners

LOCATION	From Highway 260, turn west on Turkey Track (Circle K convenience store on corner). Stay on Turkey Track to the bottom of the hill and the last house on the left.
OPEN	All year
DESCRIPTION	A 1993 country ranch bordering the National Forest with American pine primitive antiques.
NO. OF ROOMS	One room with private bathroom and two rooms share one bedroom.
RATES	Year-round rates for a single or a double with a private bathroom are $50, and a single or a double with a shared bathroom is $45. There is no minimum stay and the innkeepers require 48 hours cancellation notice for a full refund.
CREDIT CARDS	MasterCard, Visa
BREAKFAST	Full breakfast is served in the dining room and include eggs or pancakes or French toast, meat or breakfast casserole, fresh fruit, juice and coffees.
AMENITIES	Great room, refrigerator, laundry facilities and grill.
RESTRICTIONS	No smoking, no pets, all children are welcome. The two dogs, Tiger and Patches will bark when the doorbell rings, "but are immediately your friend."

THE COLDSTREAM BED & BREAKFAST

3042 Mark Twain Drive, Pinetop, AZ 85935   520-369-0115
Jeff & Cindy Northup, Resident Owners
Limited Spanish and German

LOCATION	Travel one mile south of Pinetop on Highway 260, turn left on Bucksprings Road. Go east 1.5 miles to Mark Twain Drive and turn right, the inn is on the right.
OPEN	All year
DESCRIPTION	1920 two-story "non-specific" with 19th century country furnishings…after having to type the word 'Victorian' so many times it was a treat when an innkeeper called their architectural style, "non-specific." …thanks for the originality…TI
NO. OF ROOMS	Five rooms with private bathrooms. The innkeepers suggest McNary Room as their best.
RATES	High season, November 15 through April 1, rates for a single or a double with a private bathroom are $105 to $125. Off season, April 2 through November 14, rates for a single or a double with a private bathroom are $95 to $115. There is a minimum stay on Thanksgiving, Christmas and New Years and cancellation requires seven days notice.
CREDIT CARDS	MasterCard, Visa
BREAKFAST	Full breakfast is served in the dining room and includes a choice of 30 different menus plus juices, homemade breads, coffee, tea and fruit. Lunch and dinner can be catered to groups renting the entire B&B for meetings, etc.
AMENITIES	Hot tub, robes, afternoon tea, horse boarding, pool table, TV/VCR, fireplace, bicycles, board games and "worry box" where you deposit your worries in the box and they will not bother you during your stay, "No one will take them, and you can pick them up as you leave, if you wish."…Great idea, we need a 'deadline box' here at the publishing house. … TI
RESTRICTIONS	No smoking, no pets, children over 10 are welcome.
REVIEWED	*Fodor's - The Southwest*

THE MEADOWS INN

453 North Woodland Road, Lakeside, AZ 85929   520-367-8200
Brad & Nicole Edgington and   FAX 520-367-0334
Steve & Ruth McBray, Resident Owners

LOCATION	Turn right off of Highway 260 on to Woodland, first left off of Woodland Road.
OPEN	All year
DESCRIPTION	A 1993 contemporary with French country furnishings, on eight acres.
NO. OF ROOMS	Seven rooms with private bathrooms. Nicole recommends Room #7.
RATES	Year-round rates for a single or a double with a private bathroom are $70 to $155 and suites are $115 to $155 depending on the season, There is a minimum stay on the weekends and holidays and cancellation requires 14 days notice.
CREDIT CARDS	Amex, Discover, MasterCard, Visa
BREAKFAST	Full breakfast is served in the dining room or guestroom and includes a choice of three entrees, juices, coffee, teas and breakfast breads.
AMENITIES	Wine bar and outdoor dining, use of mountain bikes, cordials and desserts for turn-downs, video and book library.
RESTRICTIONS	No smoking except in wine bar, no pets
MEMBER	Professional Association of Innkeepers International
KUDOS/COMMENTS	"Brand new (1995) inn with seven beautiful rooms and a restaurant."

MT. LEMMON

The highest peak of the Santa Catalina Mountains, northeast of Tucson via the Mt. Lemmon Highway. There is good skiing at Mt. Lemmon Ski Valley and Sabino Canyon is worth the trip, especially during a full moon.

ASPEN TRAIL BED & BREAKFAST

11120 East Miami, Mt. Lemmon, AZ 85619   *520-576-1558*
Alex & Char Carrillo, Resident Owners
Spanish spoken

LOCATION	Northeast Tucson to Catalina Highway to Summer Haven to Mt. Lemmon. Ask for a map when you make reservations.
OPEN	All year
DESCRIPTION	A 1979 two-story log cabin that was remodeled in 1993 and furnished with country antiques.
NO. OF ROOMS	Three rooms with private bathrooms. Try the Honeymoon Suite.
RATES	Year-round rates for a single or a double with a private bathroom are $140 to $160 (that includes breakfast and dinner). There is no minimum stay.
CREDIT CARDS	MasterCard, Visa
BREAKFAST	Full breakfast is served in the dining room or on the deck, and includes a fruit dish, fresh muffins or breads, egg and meat dish, potatoes, juice, cereals, toast and coffee. Dinner is also included in the price of the room.
AMENITIES	Two person spas and fireplaces in bedrooms, meeting room, living room with fireplace, big screen TV and VCR, handicapped access, many hiking trails.
RESTRICTIONS	No smoking, no pets, children over 14 will "be considered."

ORACLE

An old mining town on the northern edge of the Catalina Mountains, 35 miles northeast of Tucson via Highway 77. Great birdwatching area.

TRIANGLE L RANCH BED & BREAKFAST

2805 North Triangle L Ranch Road, Oracle, AZ 85623   520-896-2804
Tom & Margot Beeston, Resident Owners   FAX 520-896-9070
Spanish spoken

LOCATION	From Highway 77 exit to the town of Oracle, drive 1/4 mile to Circle K market. Turn left on Rockcliff, cross Highway 77, turn right on Oracle Ranch Road. Go 1/4 mile to Triangle L Ranch Road.
OPEN	September 1 through May 31.
DESCRIPTION	1880 Southwestern adobe homestead on 80 acres with original ranch furnishings and family Victorian pieces.
NO. OF ROOMS	Four cottages with private bathrooms. Pick the Trobridge Suite.
RATES	Year-round rates for a single or a double with a private bathroom are $65 to $95. There is no minimum and "we appreciate seven days notice" for cancellation.
CREDIT CARDS	Discover, MasterCard, Visa
BREAKFAST	Full breakfast served in kitchen or on front porch of main house includes fresh eggs from ranch hens, homemade baked goods, fresh fruit, French toast or pancakes, breakfast meat, juice, coffee, tea.
AMENITIES	One cottage with fireplace & private patio and three cottages with kitchens, fresh flowers in rooms, wood-burning stove in main house.
RESTRICTIONS	No smoking, no pets, all children are welcome. The resident dogs are Clancy and Rory, the cats are Dreamsicle, Catalina and Iris.
REVIEWED	*Arizona Traveler's Handbook, Fodor's Arizona, Hidden Southwest, America's Wonderful Little Hotels & Inns, Best of Arizona, Ultimate Arizona, Best Places to Stay in Arizona*
MEMBER	Arizona Association of Bed & Breakfast Inns, Professional Association of Innkeepers International
KUDOS/COMMENTS	"A special place, marvelous feeling to it and lovely hosts."

VILLA CARDINALE

1315 West Oracle Ranch Road, Oracle, AZ 85623   520-896-2516
Glenn Velardi, Resident Owner

PAGE

From Flagstaff, 130 miles north via Highway 89 on the northwest edge of the Navajo Reservation. Atop Mason Mesa overlooking Lake Powell and the Glen Canyon Dam, this is a major center for rafting, boating and excursions into the Glen Canyon National Recreation Area. Please note that we don't list B&B addresses because of a city ordinance that makes it illegal to advertise the locations of B&Bs...a stupid ordinance.

A PLACE ABOVE THE CLIFF

PO Box 2456, Page, AZ 86040   *520-645-3162*
Paula Barr, Resident Owner

KUDOS/COMMENTS   "East view of cliffs and canyons."

A ROOM WITH A VIEW, A B&B HOMESTAY

PO Box 2155, Page, AZ 86040   520-645-5763
Ken & Marilee Earlywine, Resident Owners
Some German spoken

LOCATION	In the residential section of Page.
OPEN	April 15 through October 15
DESCRIPTION	A two-story 1992 stucco and tile home with Southwestern to country English furnishings.
NO. OF ROOMS	Two rooms with private bathrooms. Obviously pick the room with the view.
RATES	Seasonal rates for a single or a double with a private bathroom are $55 to $80. There is no minimum stay and there is a cancellation policy.
CREDIT CARDS	No
BREAKFAST	Continental Plus is served in the dining room and includes juice, fresh fruit cup, toast, muffins, cereals, milk, coffee, tea and choice of egg dishes.
AMENITIES	Beverages served in the late afternoon, chocolates/candy in rooms, TV/telephone available on request, 6ft oversized tub in Rose Room.
RESTRICTIONS	No smoking except on deck of room with the view, no pets, children of any age are welcome. Mitsy is the cat and Benny is the dog and both are not allowed in the guest rooms.
KUDOS/COMMENTS	"Spectacular west view of mesas, desert panorama."

AMIE ANN'S BED & BREAKFAST

PO Box 2262, Page, AZ 86040   520-645-5505
Janet Young, Resident Owner

ANTIQUE ARBOR

PO Box 3172, Page, AZ 86040   520-645-9518
Jenny & Les Foshay, Resident Owners
Some Spanish and German spoken

LOCATION	In the residential section of Page.
OPEN	All year
DESCRIPTION	A 1977 ranch style home with antique furnishings in the guest area.
NO. OF ROOMS	Two rooms with private bathrooms and one room shares one bathroom. Pick the Blue Room.
RATES	High season, late May through early October, rates for a single or a double with a private bathroom are $75, a single or a double with a shared bathroom is $65-$70. Winter, mid-October to mid-May, rates for a single or a double with a private bathroom are $45, a single or a double with a shared bathroom is $40. There is no minimum stay and cancellation requires seven days notice.
CREDIT CARDS	No
BREAKFAST	Full breakfast is served in the dining room and includes all you can eat cold style, 3 to 5 fruits, 3 to 5 breads, pastries, cheese, 5 to 7 cereals, juices, teas and coffee, eggs and bacon on request.
AMENITIES	Cactus garden, organic garden, play yard for children, piano, exercise equipment, BBQ
RESTRICTIONS	None, the resident cat is called Miss Minnie.

EDIE'S BED & BREAKFAST

PO Box 3701, Page, AZ 86040   520-645-2754
Edie Depew, Resident Owner

HIBBERT HOMESTAY

PO Box 2526, Page, AZ 86040   520-645-9690
Les & Helen Hibbert, Resident Owners
Some Spanish and French spoken

LOCATION	In the residential section of Page.
OPEN	Always open April through October, variable winter schedule.
DESCRIPTION	A 1983 ranch style host home with Southwestern furnishings.
NO. OF ROOMS	One room with private hall bathroom.
RATES	Year-round rates for a single or a double with a private bathroom are $60 to $65. There is no minimum stay and cancellation requires seven days notice.
CREDIT CARDS	MasterCard, Visa
BREAKFAST	Continental Plus is served in the dining room and includes southwestern fare, fruit and juices and sometimes there is a full breakfast.
AMENITIES	Cable TV, fruit and snacks in room, air conditioning, coffee maker, books and games.
RESTRICTIONS	No smoking indoors, no pets, one child only in the room. The resident cats are Punker and Cleo.

HUMMER'S BED & BREAKFAST

PO Box 3532, Page, AZ 86040   520-645-2558
Paul & Diane Ostapuk, Resident Owner

LOCATION	In the residential section of Page.
OPEN	All year
DESCRIPTION	New (1994) two-story stucco with contemporary furnishings.
NO. OF ROOMS	One room with private bathroom.
RATES	Year-round rates for a single or a double with a private bathroom are $65. There is no minimum stay and cancellation requires 24 hours notice.
CREDIT CARDS	No
BREAKFAST	Full breakfast is served in the dining room, kitchen or patio and includes bacon, eggs, fresh fruit, toast, bagels, hashbrowns, coffee and juice.
AMENITIES	TV/VCR, movies of surrounding landscape, books on the region, digital piano in dining room, private entrance.
RESTRICTIONS	No smoking except on the patio, no pets. There are two outside rabbits and "hummingbirds in season!"

SUITE DREAMS

PO Box 1362, Page, AZ 86040   520-645-3145
Gracie Burton, Resident Owner

LOCATION	In the residential section of Page.
OPEN	April 1 to October 31
DESCRIPTION	A 1990 New England home with modern furnishings.
NO. OF ROOMS	One room with private bathroom.
RATES	Seasonal rates for a single or a double with a private bathroom are $65 to $75. There is no minimum stay and cancellation requires 24 hours.
CREDIT CARDS	No
BREAKFAST	Continental Plus is stocked in a refrigerator in the room and includes homemade muffins, bread, cheese, jams, two juices, milk, coffee and cereal.
AMENITIES	Telephone, TV, flowers, on weekends guest are often invited to go boating on Lake Powell with the owners.
RESTRICTIONS	No smoking, European children welcome.

THATCHER'S BED & BREAKFAST

PO Box 421, Page, AZ 86040g   520-645-3335
Neta Thatcher, Resident Owner

PATAGONIA

This important horse, cattle and farming region is also for the birds. More than 275 species are at home in the Patagonia-Sonoita Creek Sanctuary, along with other Wildlife. There's good fishing at Patagonia Lake State Park. From Tucson, 60 miles south via I-10, and 19 miles northeast of Nogales.

THE DUQUESNE HOUSE BED & BREAKFAST

357 Duquesne Street, Patagonia, AZ 85624   520-394-2732
Regina C. Medley, Resident Owner

LOCATION	In Patagonia (Great book, maybe a good name for a B&B...Inn Patagonia...I'll just go back to typing...TI) on Duquesne between Third and Fourth Avenue.
OPEN	All year
DESCRIPTION	A turn-of-the-century Southwestern adobe with brick floors and exposed beam interior.
NO. OF ROOMS	Three rooms with private bathrooms. Regina said the Red Room is her best.
RATES	Year-round rates for a single or a double are $65. There is no minimum stay and cancellation requires 14 days notice.
CREDIT CARDS	No
BREAKFAST	Full breakfast is served in the dining room and includes a main dish such as crustless quiche or apple-walnut pancakes, fresh fruit, juice, homemade rolls, coffee or tea.
AMENITIES	Woodburning stoves in two suites, fresh flowers in season, each unit has a sitting room and private entry, handicapped accessible.
RESTRICTIONS	No smoking, no pets. The resident Border Collie is Shasha and the Cairn Terriers are Negs, Corny and Thorney, the cats are Tiger and Osa.
REVIEWED	*Fodor's - the Southwest*
KUDOS/COMMENTS	"Run by an artist, charming touches and comfortable."... "Very cozy, clean, good food."

LITTLE HOUSE BED & BREAKFAST

341 Sonoita Avenue, Patagonia, AZ 85624   520-394-2493
Don & Doris Wenig, Resident Owners

LOCATION	One block north of Highway 82, between 3rd & 4th Streets.
OPEN	All year
DESCRIPTION	1985 rural Southwestern stucco over adobe guesthouse furnished with Southwestern folk art.
NO. OF ROOMS	One guesthouse with two rooms, private bathrooms, sitting areas and patio.
RATES	Year-round rates for a single or a double with a private bathroom are $60 to $80. There is no minimum stay and cancellation requires 14 days notice for full refund.
CREDIT CARDS	No
BREAKFAST	Full breakfast served in the dining room includes fresh ground coffee, fresh fruit in season, home baked breads, country fresh eggs, homemade jams and sausages.
AMENITIES	Coffee or favorite beverage delivered to the room before breakfast, privacy, no phones, no sign on the street, collection of Southwest books and cassette player in each room.
RESTRICTIONS	No smoking, no pets, inquire about children. The resident cat is called Patches.
REVIEWED	*Bed & Breakfast USA*

PATIO BED & BREAKFAST

277 McKeown Avenue, Patagonia, AZ 85624   520-394-2671
Kathy Lundy, Resident Owner

LOCATION	On the Plaza in greater downtown Patagonia.
OPEN	All year
DESCRIPTION	A 1920s southwestern and cottage with "homey" furnishings.
NO. OF ROOMS	Two rooms and a cottage with private bathrooms. Kathy picked the Cottage as her best room.
RATES	Year-round rates for a single or a double with a private bathroom are $60, the cottage is $75. There is no minimum stay or reservation/cancellation policy.
CREDIT CARDS	No
BREAKFAST	Full breakfast is served in Kathy's home where she specializes in sourdough pancakes and blueberry muffins, or guests may eat at the restaurant on the Plaza as part of the room rate.
AMENITIES	Always a plate of homemade cookies for guests and rooms are wheelchair accessible.
RESTRICTIONS	No smoking.

PAULDEN

Paulden is 36 miles north of Prescott on Highway 89, surrounded by the Prescott National Forest.

DOUBLE D RANCH & WAGON TRAIN COMPANY

111 Barbara Road, Paulden, AZ 86334   520-636-0418
D. Dipietro, Resident Owner

LOCATION	Guests need to meet hosts at Paulden mini-mart for escort to the ranch.
OPEN	All year
DESCRIPTION	1981 remodeled rammed-earth adobe with Southwestern furnishings.
NO. OF ROOMS	One room with private bathroom, covered wagons available for extra guests.
RATES	Year-round rates for a single or double with a private bathroom are $139 to $199. There is no minimum stay and there is a cancellation policy.
CREDIT CARDS	MasterCard, Visa
BREAKFAST	Full breakfast is served in the dining room or in bed. All other meals are included in the price of the room.
AMENITIES	Cross-country horseback riding, champagne breakfast for two, fresh flowers in room, can sleep in 100 year old covered wagon.
RESTRICTIONS	No smoking, no pets, children over 10 are welcome. There are two resident dogs Lobo and Ronco, two barn cats, the rooster Arnold, the burro Cisco and lots of horses.

PAYSON

This mountain community surrounded by forests and the awesome Mogollon Rim, is an easy beeline 78 miles north of Mesa via Highway 87 (the Beeline Highway). Natural and other wonders include the Tonto Natural Bridge, Payson Zoo, Zane Grey's Cabin, and all the Paul Bunyans at the State Championship Loggers and Sawdust Festival in July.

CHELCIE INN

208 East Bonita, Payson, AZ 85547   520-474-6525
Ed & Jay Waldron, Resident Owners

GRANDMA'S PLACE

305 West Forest Drive, Payson, AZ 85541   520-472-6362
Dick Young, Resident Owner

SUMMIT PLACE

716 West Summit, Payson, AZ 85541   520-474-6752
C.R. Pritchard, Resident Owner

PHOENIX

Desert mountains form the skyline of Arizona's state capitol and largest city. This is a major cosmopolitan, cultural and industrial center of the Southwest and a winter haven for snowbirds. Accessible via major highways from all directions.

DESERTFARREN "PRIVATE" HACIENDA

PO Box 5550, Carefree, AZ 85377   602-488-1110
Larry Farren, Resident Owner   FAX 620-488-1500
Spanish and some German, Italian and Swedish spoken

LOCATION	Directions and map with reservation confirmation.
OPEN	All year
DESCRIPTION	Mission Hacienda adobe, brick and oak interior, on 20 acres.
NO. OF ROOMS	Three rooms with private bathrooms and one room shares one bathroom. Pick the Deer Room.
RATES	High season, October through May, rates for a single or a double with a private bathroom are $139, suites start at $163 and the entire B&B rents for $500. Off season, June through September, rates for a single or a double with a private bathroom are from $69, suites are from $99 and the entire B&B rents for $299. There is a minimum stay on holidays and there is a cancellation policy.
CREDIT CARDS	Amex, MasterCard, Visa
BREAKFAST	Continental Plus
AMENITIES	Hot tub and swimming pool, flowers in room, robes, TV/VCR, afternoon munchies, full concierge services, meeting facilities, massage, hiking trails, mountain bikes, large common area with fireplaces.
RESTRICTIONS	No pets, smoking outside

HACIENDA ALTA

5750 East Camelback Road, Phoenix, AZ 85018   602-945-8525
Margaret & Ed Newhall, Resident Owner

Ot34 Sut on arrival

MARICOPA MANOR
BED & BREAKFAST INN

15 West Pasadena Avenue, Phoenix, AZ 85013   602-274-6302
Mary Ellen & Paul Kelley, Resident Owners

LOCATION	One block north of Camelback Road off Central Avenue, five miles from the center of Phoenix… please define the center of Phoenix…TI
OPEN	All Year
DESCRIPTION	1928 Spanish-Mission style with antique furnishings
NO. OF ROOMS	Seven suites with private bathrooms. Paul recommends the Library Suite…which he will book for you…TI…(sorry, it's been a long day.)
RATES	High season, September through May, rates for a single or a double are $99 to $159. Off season, June through August, rates for a single or a double are $79 to $129. There is no minimum stay and cancellation requires seven days notice and a $15 cancellation fee.
CREDIT CARDS	Amex, Discover, MasterCard, Visa
BREAKFAST	Continental Plus is served in the suite and includes fresh fruit and juice, homemade breads, quiche and coffee, etc.
AMENITIES	Spa, flowers, robes, cable TV, phones.
RESTRICTIONS	No smoking, no pets.
REVIEWED	*America's Wonderful Little Hotels & Inns, Special Places, Recommended Inns of the Southwest, Fodor's - The Southwest*
MEMBER	Professional Association of Innkeepers International, American Association of Historic Inns, Arizona Association of Bed & Breakfast Inns
RATED	AAA 3 Diamonds, Mobil 3 Stars
KUDOS/COMMENTS	"An oasis in the center of Phoenix, large, comfortable suite rooms."

VALLEY O' THE SUN BED & BREAKFAST

PO Box 2214, Scottsdale, AZ 85252   *602-941-1281*
Kay Curtis, Resident Owner

LOCATION	In north Tempe, near Arizona State University, the cross streets are College Drive and McKellips Road. Exact directions are given in reservation confirmation letter.
OPEN	All year
DESCRIPTION	1960 ranch with traditional furnishings.
NO. OF ROOMS	Two rooms share one bathroom.
RATES	Year-round rates for a single or a double with a shared bathroom are $25 to $35. There is a $10 surcharge for a one night stay and 24 hour cancellation policy with a $15 cancellation fee.
CREDIT CARDS	No
BREAKFAST	Continental breakfast is served in the dining room and includes fresh fruit in season or fruit juice, Danish, muffins, cold cereal, coffee and tea.
AMENITIES	TV/radio in rooms.
RESTRICTIONS	No smoking (limited to the patio), no pets, children over 10 are welcome.

PINE

What a difference 15 miles can make, because that is just how close this wonderful little town is to Phoenix via Highway 87 north. Visit the Tonto Natural Bridge, the Pine/Strawberry Museum and the Fossil Creek Springs.

WINEBRENNER'S BED & BREAKFAST

38 Pine Creek Canyon Road, Pine, AZ 85544   520-476-3843
Cork & Sandy Winebrenner, Resident Owners

LOCATION	Go to the northeast end of Pine, on Pine Creek Road, turn beside Mormon Church just above Texaco and go about .5 mile up Pine Creek.
OPEN	All year
DESCRIPTION	A 1989 chalet with country and folk art furnishings.
NO. OF ROOMS	One room with private bathroom.
RATES	Year-round rates for a single or a double with a private bathroom are $75 to $95. Rates are higher on holiday weekends. There is a minimum stay on holiday weekends and cancellation requires seven days notice with a $10. fee.
CREDIT CARDS	No, cash only.
BREAKFAST	Full breakfast is served in the dining room, guestroom or outside and includes French toast with homemade jams and sauces, quiche, muffins and biscuits.
AMENITIES	Private entrance, guests are offered a homemade dessert and beverage in the evening of one night of their stay.
RESTRICTIONS	No smoking, no pets, no children. The resident terrier mix is called Sneakers...good name for a terrier...TI

PORTAL

The entrance to Cave Creek Canyon, another choice bird-watching area and nesting place of the Elegant Trogon. In the Chiricahua Wilderness Area and Coronado National Forest, at the southeast corner of the state, 67 miles north of Douglas and the U.S./ Mexico border via Highway 80. *

THE GEORGE WALKER HOUSE

HCR Box 74, Portal, AZ 85632   520-558-2287
Dale & Michael Julian, Resident Owners

LOCATION	From Tucson take I-10 east to Portal Road, exit 382. Go straight on Portal Road for 20 miles. Do not bear left at Foothills Road. As you enter Paradise, pass mailboxes, three houses, two corrals and tiny adobe to the sign on the right.
OPEN	From March 1 through November 31st.
DESCRIPTION	A 1902 rustic mining town cabin with comfortable eclectic furnishings.
NO. OF ROOMS	Two rooms share one bathroom. The east bedroom is the best.
RATES	Year-round rates for a single or a double with a shared bathroom are $45 to $55. The entire B&B rents for $75 to $100. There is no minimum stay and cancellation requires two weeks notice.
CREDIT CARDS	No
BREAKFAST	This is a "self-serve" B&B with a pantry that includes coffee, teas, breakfast cereal, juice and canned "camp grub."
AMENITIES	The innkeepers cater to birders. There is an extensive library of field guides, maps and video tapes of Southeastern Arizona's "specialty" birds. Ten bird feeders are on the property and a species list is available.
RESTRICTIONS	No smoking (porch only), no pets. The resident Lab/Heeler is called Blackie and is confined to the innkeeper's private yard.

PRESCOTT

Once the territorial capitol, this mile-high city is the place to be for a taste of the old west: Territorial Prescott Days in June and its famous Frontier Days Celebration in July is the nation's oldest rodeo. Amazing but true is the Governor's Cup Ralley in October, an antique car marathon to the Grand Canyon. Surrounded by the Prescott National Forest, 93 miles northwest of Phoenix via I-17 and Highway 69.

BRIAR WREATH INN B&B

232 South Arizona Street, Prescott, AZ 86303   520-778-6048
Bill & Colleen Neuman, Resident Owners

LOCATION	One and a half blocks south of Gurley Street, six blocks east of Court House Square.
OPEN	All year
DESCRIPTION	A 1904 Craftsman Bungalow with European country furnishings.
NO. OF ROOMS	Two rooms with private bathrooms. Pick the Tuscany Room that has 12 windows.
RATES	Year-round rates for a single or a double with a private bathroom are $65 to $90. There is a two day minimum stay on holidays and special event weekends. Cancellation requires five days notice.
CREDIT CARDS	No
BREAKFAST	Full breakfast is served in the dining room includes fresh fruit, meat and egg dish or meat and pancakes, muffins, toast, juice, coffee or other beverages.
AMENITIES	Evening hors d'oeuvres, hot and cold beverages always available, library and fireplace in Great Room, antique grand piano, outside sitting area, goldfish pond, TV available on request.
RESTRICTIONS	No smoking, no pets, children over 12 are welcome. Barkley is the dog and Maggie is the Norwegian Forest Cat...What is a Norwegian Forest Cat?...TI
AWARDS	Honorable mention as a Waverly Room of the Year, *Country Inns Magazine*, October 1994.

HASSAYAMPA INN

122 East Gurley Street, Prescott, AZ 86301
Bill & Georgia Teich, Resident Owners
Some Spanish spoken

520-778-9434
800-322-1927
FAX 520-778-9434

LOCATION	Center of town, corner of Marina and Gurley Streets.
OPEN	All year
DESCRIPTION	1927 four-story, restored Spanish Colonial Revival with antique furnishings. On the National Historic Register.
NO. OF ROOMS	Sixty-eight rooms with private bathrooms. The owners suggest the Balcony Suite.
RATES	High season, April through October, rates for a single or a double with a private bathroom are $99 to $119, suites are $150 to $175. Off season, November through March, rates for a single or a double with a private bathroom are $89 to $109, suites are $135 to $160. There is no minimum stay and cancellation requires 48 hours notice.
CREDIT CARDS	Amex, Carte Blanche, Diners Club, Discover, MasterCard, Visa
BREAKFAST	Full breakfast is served in dining room and can be chosen from the menu. Lunch and dinner are also available in full service restaurant.
AMENITIES	Evening cocktail, telephone and TV in rooms, fireplace and grand piano in lobby, champagne and chocolates in room, meeting rooms and handicapped access.
RESTRICTIONS	No pets
REVIEWED	*Country Inns - The Southwest, Hidden Southwest, 50 Romantic Getaways*
RATED	AAA 1 Diamond

Smoking?

JUNIPER WELL RANCH
BED & BREAKFAST

Contreras & Tonto Roads, Prescott, AZ 86304　　　　　520-442-3415
David Bonham, Resident Owners
Spanish spoken

LOCATION	Twelve miles northwest of Prescott at Tonto & Contreras Roads in the Wescott National Forest. No street address, please call for directions.
OPEN	All year
DESCRIPTION	A 1975 ranch house and two modern log cabins on a 50 acre horse ranch.
NO. OF ROOMS	The two log cabins sleep four and six and the ranch house sleeps up to 10. All bedrooms have private bathrooms.
RATES	Year-round rate for a single or a double with a private bathroom is $105. There is no minimum stay and cancellation requires one week notice.
CREDIT CARDS	Amex, Discover, MasterCard, Visa
BREAKFAST	Full breakfast is served in the guestrooms and includes coffee, milk, juices, pastry, English muffins, eggs, pancakes, and assorted beverages. Steak cookouts by arrangement.
AMENITIES	Guests can help feed the horses, outdoor hot tub, cookouts, hiking and birdwatching.
RESTRICTIONS	No smoking. There are over 30 horses on the ranch, some Llamas and Queensland Heeler by the name of Happy. David alleges that Happy speaks Spanish…We'll need guest confirmation on this…TI

LYNX CREEK FARM BED & BREAKFAST

PO Box 4301, Prescott, AZ 86302   520-778-9573
Greg & Wendy Temple, Resident Owners

LOCATION	Five miles east of Prescott on Lynx Creek, directions with reservation confirmation.
OPEN	All year
DESCRIPTION	1980 guesthouse and 1992 two story log cabin with country antique furnishings.
NO. OF ROOMS	Six rooms with private bathrooms. Wendy suggests the Chaparral Room.
RATES	High season, March through December, rates for a single or double with a private bathroom are $85 to $120 and suites are $105 to $140. Off season, January through February, rates for a single or a double with a private bathroom are $75 to $110, suites are $95 to $130. There is no minimum stay and cancellation requires 10 days notice with a 15% charge.
CREDIT CARDS	Amex, Discover, MasterCard, Visa
BREAKFAST	Full breakfast is served in dining room and includes fresh eggs and milk from the farm and fruits and vegetables from the orchard and garden…Yum…TK
AMENITIES	Homemade cookies at check-in, complimentary cream sherry in rooms, robes, wood stoves, hot tubs on decks, hors d' oeuvres and cocktails in the evening, kitchenettes.
RESTRICTIONS	No smoking. Well-behaved children and pets are welcome. Three resident dogs, six cats, two goats, chickens, two pigs, geese and exotic birds.
REVIEWED	*Best Places to Stay in the Southwest*
AWARDS	"Best Bed & Breakfast in Arizona" Arizona Republic 1994.

MARKS HOUSE VICTORIAN BED & BREAKFAST

203 East Union Street, Prescott, AZ 86303   520-778-4632
Dottie & Harold Viehweg, Managers

LOCATION	Entering Prescott, stay on Gurley Street to the light at Marina Street and turn left one block. The inn is on the corner of Marina and Union Streets, one block east of the Court House Square.
OPEN	All year
DESCRIPTION	An 1894 two-story Queen Anne Victorian Painted Lady furnished with period antiques. Listed on the National and State Historic Registers.
NO. OF ROOMS	Four rooms with private bathrooms. Dottie recommends the Queen Anne Suite.
RATES	Year-round rates for a single or a double with a private bathroom are $75 to $120. The suite is $135. There is a minimum stay on holidays and during special events. The innkeepers require seven days notice for cancellation and 14 days notice for holidays and special events.
CREDIT CARDS	Discover, MasterCard, Visa
BREAKFAST	Full breakfast is served in the dining room and includes juice, fruit, main entree, muffins or fruit breads, coffee, tea and cocoa. Full Thanksgiving dinner for guests is $15 a person.
AMENITIES	Hors d'oeuvres in the afternoon, flavored soda in the room and a split of wine for special events like anniversaries, weddings, etc.
RESTRICTIONS	No smoking (if disregarded the innkeepers charge a cleaning fee of $100) no pets, no children. The resident mini-poodle is called Pierre.
REVIEWED	*Fodor's - The Southwest*
MEMBER	Arizona Bed & Breakfast Association, Prescott Bed & Breakfast Association
RATED	Mobil 3 Stars
AWARDS	Featured in the August 1994 *Good Housekeeping* as one of the 29 Best B&B Inns in the United States.
KUDOS/COMMENTS	"Nice Victorian."

MT. VERNON INN

204 North Mount Vernon Avenue, Prescott, AZ 86301   520-778-0886
John & Sybil Nelson, Resident Owners   FAX 520-778-7305

LOCATION	From Highways 69 and 89 entering Prescott on Gurley, go one mile north of Gurley, turn right on Mount Vernon at the third signal after entering Prescott; located in the Historic District.
OPEN	All year
DESCRIPTION	A two-story 1900 Victorian Gothic with Victorian and contemporary furnishings and guesthouses.
NO. OF ROOMS	Four rooms with private bathrooms. Sybil picked Avalon as her best room. Three cottages do not include breakfast in the room rate.
RATES	High season, May through December, rates for a single or a double with a private bathroom are $90 to $100. The guesthouses are $90 to $110. Off season, January through April, rates for a single or a double with a private bathroom are $75 to $90. The guesthouses are $80 to $100. There is a two-night minimum stay on holiday weekends and cancellation requires 72 hours notice.
CREDIT CARDS	Amex, Discover, MasterCard, Visa
BREAKFAST	Continental Plus is served in the main house dining room and includes fresh fruit, homemade granolas, freshly baked breads and muffins.
AMENITIES	Telephones in each room, TV/VCR and videos in sitting room, refreshments in the afternoon, fireplace in the sitting room.
RESTRICTIONS	No smoking, children are welcome in cottages only. Niki is the dog and Abby is the cat.
REVIEWED	American Historic Inns, Complete Guide to American B&Bs.
MEMBER	Professional Association of Innkeepers International Arizona Association of Bed & Breakfast Inns.
RATED	AAA 2 Diamonds
KUDOS/COMMENTS	"Nice Victorian"

downtown ✗

PLEASANT STREET INN

142 South Pleasant Street, Prescott, AZ 86303   520-445-4774
Jean B. Urban, Resident Owner

LOCATION	Two blocks south of Gurley Street and three blocks due east of Courthouse Square.
OPEN	All year
DESCRIPTION	A 1906 two story Victorian with English traditional furnishings.
NO. OF ROOMS	Four rooms with private bathrooms. Pick the Pineview Suite
RATES	Year-round rates for a single or a double with a private bathroom are $80 to $120, the suites are $110 to $120. There is a two day minimum for holidays and local events and cancellation requires seven days notice.
CREDIT CARDS	Discover, MasterCard, Visa
BREAKFAST	Full breakfast is served in the dining room and includes fresh fruit dish, homemade breads and muffins, entree and breakfast meat.
AMENITIES	Fresh flowers in each room, afternoon hors d'oeuvres and refreshments.
RESTRICTIONS	No smoking, no pets
RATED	AAA 2 Diamonds
KUDOS/COMMENTS	"Beautifully remodeled 1900s home decorated in Ethan Allen."

PRESCOTT COUNTRY INN BED & BREAKFAST

503 South Montezuma Street, Prescott, AZ 86303   520-445-7991
Wendy Ostermeyer, Resident Manager

PRESCOTT PINES INN BED & BREAKFAST

901 White Spar Road, Prescott, AZ 86303   520-445-7270
Cindy & Harry Miner, Managers

downtown

VICTORIAN INN OF PRESCOTT

246 South Cortez, Prescott, AZ 86303   520-778-2642
Tamia Thunstedt, Resident Owner   800-704-2642

LOCATION	One block from historic Town Square
OPEN	All Year
DESCRIPTION	1893 Queen Anne Victorian with antique furnishings.
NO. OF ROOMS	One suite with private bathroom. Three rooms with shared bathrooms. Pick the Victorian Suite.
RATES	Year-round rates for a single or a double with a private bathroom are $135 to $145 and the rate for a single or a double with a shared bathroom is $80 to $95. There is no minimum stay and cancellation requires 48 hours notice.
CREDIT CARDS	Amex, Discover, MasterCard, Visa
BREAKFAST	Full breakfast is served in dining room
RESTRICTIONS	No smoking. No pets. Children over five are welcome.
REVIEWED	*Recommended Country Inns of Arizona, New Mexico & Texas*
MEMBER	Arizona Association of B&B Inns
AWARDS	"Best in State 1992," *Arizona Republic*
KUDOS/COMMENTS	"Very 'Victorian' with authentic period pieces."

SAFFORD

Located on Highway 70, 40 miles west of the New Mexico border, Safford is close to Roper Lake State Park and the Coronado National Forest.

OLNEY HOUSE BED & BREAKFAST

1104 Central Avenue, Safford, AZ 85546   520-428-5118
Patrick & Carol Mahoney, Resident Owners   800-814-5118
Spanish and some Hindi, Thai, Nepali and Baha Indonesian spoken.

LOCATION	From Highway 70 go right on Central Avenue and then two blocks to the corner of 11th and Central Avenue.
OPEN	All year
DESCRIPTION	An 1890 two-story Western Colonial Revival decorated with masks, carpets and carvings from Central and Southeast Asia. On the National and State Historic Registers.
NO. OF ROOMS	Two cottages with private bathrooms and three rooms share one bathroom. Pick Room 3.
RATES	Year-round rates for a single or a double with a private or a shared bathroom are $70 and $10 for an additional person. There is no minimum stay and reservations are recommended.
CREDIT CARDS	MasterCard, Visa
BREAKFAST	Full breakfast is served in the dining room and includes western omelette and homefries, mueselix, yogurt, and fruit or oatmeal with pecans, wheat germ and fruit, coffee, juice, tea and milk.
AMENITIES	Outdoor spa and robes, flowers in room during season, near desert or mountain hiking, trail information, bird watching.
RESTRICTIONS	No smoking, no pets, and children must be supervised at all times. There are all sorts of wild birds around the B&B including Kestral Hawks that nest on the 2nd floor veranda.

SEDONA

In exquisite Red Rock Country, 28 miles south of Flagstaff at the junction of Highway 89A and 179. This major art colony at the southern end of Oak Creek Canyon is an eclectic mix of natural wonders, contemporary art and new age spirituality. Summer is filled with music and art festivals; the Apple Festival in October, and Festival of Lights in December. There's good fishing in Oak Creek, or meet the trout at Page Springs Hatchery. Oak Creek Canyon isn't bad either.

BED & BREAKFAST AT SADDLE ROCK RANCH

255 Rock Ridge Drive, Sedona, AZ 86336   *520-282-7640*
Fran & Dan Bruno, Resident Owners   *FAX 520-282-6829*
Italian, French, German and Spanish spoken

LOCATION	One mile from the center of Sedona, two blocks off Airport Road.
OPEN	All year
DESCRIPTION	1920s Western ranch estate with Victorian and English country furnishings, on three acres.
NO. OF ROOMS	Three rooms with private bathrooms. Fran suggests the Saddle Rock Suite.
RATES	Year-round rates for a single or a double are $105 to $135, the entire B&B rents for $375. There is a three night minimum during high season and holidays and cancellation requires 10 days notice and $15 processing fee.
CREDIT CARDS	No
BREAKFAST	Full breakfast is served in the breakfast room, dining balcony, or poolside and includes fresh-squeezed orange juice, fruit course, entree of fritata, waffle, Dutch baby or breakfast casserole and meat, fresh brewed coffee and oatmeal cookies.
AMENITIES	Robes, pool towels, fresh flowers, teddy bears, outdoor hot tub and pool, fireplaces in all rooms, TV, canopied beds, concierge services.
RESTRICTIONS	No smoking. no pets and children over 13 are welcome. The Miniature Schnauzers are Diana and Fergie.
REVIEWED	*Recommended Country Inns, the Southwest, America's Wonderful Little Hotels & Inns, Inn Places for Bed & Breakfast.*
MEMBER	Professional Association of Innkeepers International, Arizona Association of Bed & Breakfast Inns, Sedona Bed & Breakfast Innkeepers Guild
RATED	AAA 3 Diamonds, Mobil 3 Stars
KUDOS/COMMENTS	"Beautiful vista, charming hosts at historic property."

BRIAR PATCH INN

HC30, Box 1002, Sedona, AZ 86336   520-282-2342
Edward (Ike) & JoAnn Olson, Resident Owners
KUDOS/COMMENTS "Wonderful, tranquil setting, friendly staff."

CANYON VILLA BED & BREAKFAST INN

125 Canyon Circle Drive, Sedona, AZ 86351   520-284-1226
Chuck & Marion Yadon, Resident Owners   800-453-1166
                                                       FAX 520-284-2114

LOCATION	From I-17, exit Highway 179 west. Go 7.9 miles to Bell Rock Boulevard and turn left, then immediately turn right on Canyon Circle Drive.
OPEN	All year
DESCRIPTION	A 1992 two-story Spanish Mission Style inn.
NO. OF ROOMS	Eleven rooms with private bathrooms. Chuck recommends the Ocotillo Room.
RATES	Year-round rates for a single or a double with a private bathroom are $115 to $205. There is a two day minimum stay on weekends (Friday and Saturday) and cancellation requires seven days notice.
CREDIT CARDS	MasterCard, Visa
BREAKFAST	Full breakfast is served in the dining room and includes choice of two fruit juices, fruit plate, entree, choice of hot beverages all served on china and crystal.
AMENITIES	All rooms have private patios or balcony, telephone, TV, robes, individual heating and cooling, whirlpool bathtubs; library and reading garden, afternoon snacks and beverage, large heated pool, indoor and outdoor fireplaces are used during cooler times.
RESTRICTIONS	No smoking, no pets. The resident Goldie is Belle but she is confined to the owner's area.
REVIEWED	America's Wonderful Little Hotels & Inns, Fodor's - The Southwest, Recommended Country Inns - The Southwest
MEMBER	Professional Association of Innkeepers International, Arizona Association of Bed & Breakfast Inns
RATED	AAA 4 Diamonds, ABBA 4 Crowns, Mobile 4 Stars
AWARDS	ABBA's Top 16 Inns Nationwide.

KUDOS/COMMENTS "Luxurious, elegant."

THE CANYON WREN CABINS FOR TWO

Star Route 3, Box 1140, Sedona, AZ 86336　　　　　　520-282-6900
Milena Pfeifer & Mike Smith, Resident Owners　　　　800-437-9736
Slovenian spoken

LOCATION	Six miles north of Sedona on Highway 89A in Oak Creek Canyon.
OPEN	All year
DESCRIPTION	1986 log cabin and three cedar chalets with country furnishings.
NO. OF ROOMS	Four cabins with private bathrooms.
RATES	Year-round rates, except holidays, for a single or a double with a private bathroom are $125 to $135. There is a two-night minimum on weekends and three on holidays. Cancellation requires 72 hours notice.
CREDIT CARDS	MasterCard, Visa
BREAKFAST	Continental Plus includes choice of beverages, juice, fruit, homemade muffins, rolls, bagels with cream cheeses, jams and cookies.
AMENITIES	Concierge services, BBQ, flannel sheets in winter, whirlpool bathtubs, fireplaces, decks and swimming in Oak Creek.
RESTRICTIONS	No smoking, no pets, no children. The resident Queensland Heeler/Shepherd are Nasa and Stubs, mother and son.
REVIEWED	*Hidden Southwest*

CASA DE ABUELITA

41 Arrow Drive, Sedona, AZ 86336   *520-282-6241*
Mary Allison, Resident Owner   *800-854-8152*
Some Spanish and French spoken   *FAX 520-282-5636*

LOCATION	From the intersection of Highway 89A and 179 follow Highway 179 south to Arrow Drive, first house on the left.
OPEN	All year
DESCRIPTION	A contemporary ranch with separate quarters for guests.
NO. OF ROOMS	Three rooms with private bathrooms. Pick the King Room.
RATES	Year-round rates for a single or a double with a private bathroom are $100 to $150, the entire B&B rents for $300. There is a minimum stay and cancellation policy.
CREDIT CARDS	Amex, Discover, MasterCard, Visa
BREAKFAST	Full gourmet breakfast served in the Common Room includes fresh squeezed orange juice, coffee, seasonal fresh fruit, "followed by great breakfast."
AMENITIES	Complimentary hot and cold beverages, Jacuzzi in King Room, concierge services, large Common Room.
RESTRICTIONS	No smoking except on patio and gardens, no pets, children over 10 are welcome. Fred the "intelligent and gentle Australian Shepherd is restricted from the guestrooms."

CASA SEDONA

55 Hozoni Drive, Sedona, AZ 86336   520-282-2938
Misty & Lori Zitko & Dick Curtis, Resident Owners.   800-525-3756

LOCATION	Three miles west of uptown Sedona.
OPEN	All year.
DESCRIPTION	A 1993 two story Southwestern inn.
NO. OF ROOMS	Fifteen rooms with private bathrooms.
RATES	Year-round rates for a single or a double with a private bathroom are $95 to $150. There is a two night minimum stay on weekends and holidays and cancellation requires 72 hours notice.
CREDIT CARDS	Discover, MasterCard, Visa
BREAKFAST	Full breakfast is served in the dining room, guestroom or patios and includes homemade baked items, fresh fruit, juice, tea, coffee and hot cocoa with a different hot entree every morning.
AMENITIES	Fireplace in every room, plus whirlpool tub, robes, and terraces.
RESTRICTIONS	No smoking, children over 10 are welcome.
REVIEWED	*Fodor's - The Southwest, America's Wonderful Little Hotels & Inns, American & Canadian Bed & Breakfasts, Special Places*
MEMBER	Professional Association of Innkeepers International, Arizona Association of Bed & Breakfast Inns
RATED	AAA 3 Diamonds, ABBA 3 Crowns
KUDOS/COMMENTS	"Very nice, beautiful views."

CATHEDRAL ROCK LODGE

61 Los Amigos Lane, Sedona, AZ 86336   520-282-7608
Carol Shannon, Resident Owner   FAX 520-282-4505

LOCATION	From Sedona take Highway 89A southwest for 4.1 miles to Upper Red Rock Loop Road and follow the road for 2.7 miles.
OPEN	All year
DESCRIPTION	A 1948, 1952, 1963, 1993 ranch and cabin with "assorted comfortable" furnishings…great furniture description…TI
NO. OF ROOMS	Four rooms with private bathrooms.
RATES	Year-round rates for a single or a double with a private bathroom are $70 to $75, suite with a kitchen is $110 and the cabin with a kitchen is $100. There is a minimum stay on the weekend and cancellation requires seven days notice.
CREDIT CARDS	MasterCard, Visa
BREAKFAST	Full breakfast is served in the dining room and includes fresh ground coffee, assorted teas, homemade jams, hot breads plus entrees such as biscuits & gravy, waffles, etc. Continental Plus is served in the cabin.
AMENITIES	Fireplace lounge with TV/VCR, collection of movies filmed in Sedona, books, magazines and trail guides of the area, terraced gardens, BBQ, children's playhouse.
RESTRICTIONS	No smoking, no pets, all children are welcome. Shookums the cat is "assistant manager in charge of guest relations."
REVIEWED	*America's Wonderful Little Hotels & Inns Arizona Traveler's Handbook, Bed & Breakfast USA, Best of Arizona, Recommended Country Inns of the Southwest*
MEMBER	Arizona Association of Bed & Breakfast Inns, Sedona B&B Innkeepers Guild, Professional Association of Innkeepers International.

COZY CACTUS BED & BREAKFAST

80 Canyon Circle Drive, Sedona, AZ 86351   520-284-0082
Lynne & Bob Gillman, Resident Owners   800-788-2082
Italian, and American Sign Language   FAX 520-284-4210

LOCATION   Northbound from I-17 on State Road 179, 8.4 miles to Bell Rock
                     Boulevard and southbound from SR89A on Highway 179, 6.4 miles
                     to Bell Rock Boulevard. Turn west on Bell Rock Boulevard, go one
                     block, turn right to Canyon Circle Drive, 4th building on the right.

OPEN   All year

DESCRIPTION   1983 stucco ranch with contemporary and antique furnishings.

NO. OF ROOMS   Five rooms with private bathrooms. Pick the American Room.

RATES   Year-round rates for a single or a double with a private bathroom are
                     $80 to $95. The entire B&B rents for $440.

CREDIT CARDS   Discover, MasterCard, Visa

BREAKFAST   Full breakfast served in the dining room includes blueberry coconut
                     muffins, fresh fruit cup, whole wheat raspberry, buttermilk pancakes,
                     turkey sausage, coffee, tea and four juices.

AMENITIES   Afternoon refreshments, access to National Forest, bird watching,
                     nearby golf and tennis.

RESTRICTIONS   Smoking restricted to patio, no pets, all children are welcome. The
                     CockaPoo is called Fudge, and two Schnauzers, Chevis and Katie
                     are, "kept out of guest rooms."

REVIEWED   *American's Wonderful Little Hotels, Fodor's - The Southwest*

MEMBER   Professional Association of Innkeepers International, Arizona
                     Association of Bed & Breakfast Inns, Sedona Bed & Breakfast
                     Innkeepers Guild

RATED   AAA 2 Diamonds

GARLAND'S OAK CREEK LODGE

PO Box 152, Sedona, AZ 86336   602-282-3343
Mary & Gary Garland, Resident Owners

KUDOS/COMMENTS   "Fabulous food and setting, hard to get reservations."

THE GRAHAM BED & BREAKFAST INN

150 Canyon Circle Drive , Sedona, AZ 86351   520-284-1425
Carol & Roger Redenbaugh, Resident Owners   800-228-1425
Spanish & African (South African) spoken.   FAX 520-284-0767

LOCATION	From I-17 or Highway 89A go to Highway 179, turn on Bell Rock Boulevard, the inn is two blocks on the right.
OPEN	All year
DESCRIPTION	1985 contemporary Southwestern with Southwestern furnishings.
NO. OF ROOMS	Six rooms with private bathrooms. Carol recommends the Sedona Suite as her best room.
RATES	Year-round rates for a single or a double with a private bathroom are $99 to $179, a suite is $209. There is a minimum stay on most weekends and holidays and cancellation requires 14 days notice and a $15 fee.
CREDIT CARDS	Discover, MasterCard, Visa
BREAKFAST	Full "bountiful, gourmet" breakfast is served in dining room and includes cereal on a sideboard, fruit course, bread course, main course.
AMENITIES	Outdoor pool and spa, guest bicycles, fresh flowers in all rooms, TV/VCR, private balconies, robes, some rooms have Jacuzzi tubs and fireplaces, afternoon refreshments.
RESTRICTIONS	No smoking, except on room balcony, no pets, all children are welcome. The resident Lahsa Apso is called Giper and stays in the office or on the pool deck.
REVIEWED	*America's Wonderful Little Hotels & Inns, Best Places to Stay in the Southwest, Romantic Getaways, Arizona Handbook*
MEMBER	Arizona Association of B&B Innkeepers, Professional Association of Innkeepers International, Sedona B&B Innkeepers Guild
RATED	AAA 4 Diamonds, Mobil 4 Stars
KUDOS/COMMENTS	"Sedona's finest B&B, elegant rooms, beautiful views."

GREYFIRE FARM BED & BREAKFAST

1240 Jacks Canyon Road, Sedona, AZ 86336   *520-284-2340*
David J. Payne & Elaine Ross, Resident Owners   *800-579-2340*
                                                 FAX 520-284-2340

LOCATION	1-17 north to exit 298 which is Highway 179. Go seven miles to Jacks Canyon Road, turn right and go 1.7 miles to B&B.
OPEN	All year
DESCRIPTION	1980 Southwestern ranch on 2 1/2 acres with antique & contemporary furnishings.
NO. OF ROOMS	Two rooms with private bathrooms, pick the Canyon Suite.
RATES	High season, March through June, rates for a single or a double with a private bathroom are $85 to $90. Off season, January, February, July and August, rates for a single or a double with a private bathroom are $75 to $80. There is a two day minimum stay on the weekends and three days on holiday weekends. Cancellation requires seven days notice and a $15 fee.
CREDIT CARDS	MasterCard, Visa
BREAKFAST	Full breakfast served in the dining room.
AMENITIES	Accommodations for two guest horses are available.
RESTRICTIONS	No smoking, small pets welcome. There are four resident Arabians, four Australian Shepherds, and four parrots…as the innkeepers said in their survey, "Animal lovers are always welcome."
REVIEWED	*Hidden Southwest, Ultimate Arizona, Horse Lovers Vacation Guide, Romantic Getaway Guide*
MEMBER	Professional Association of Innkeepers International, Sedona Bed & Breakfast Innkeepers Guild
KUDOS/COMMENTS	"Small, very comfortable homestay on a mini-farm."

KENNEDY HOUSE BED & BREAKFAST

2075 Upper Red Rock Loop Road, Sedona, AZ 86336   *520-282-1624*
Charles & Tonya Kennedy, Resident Owners

LOCATION	From Highways 89A and 179 in Sedona go west on Highway 89A approximately four miles to Upper Red Rock Loop, then turn left and go approximately 2.2 miles to Kennedy Lane, turn right, first house on the right.
OPEN	February through December.
DESCRIPTION	1988 contemporary two-story with contemporary and country furnishings.
NO. OF ROOMS	Two rooms with private bathrooms.
RATES	Year-round rates for a single or a double with a private bathroom are $80 to $90. The entire B&B rents for $125 with a four day minimum stay. There is a two night minimum stay on the weekends and cancellation requires five days notice with a $10 per room charge.
CREDIT CARDS	Amex, MasterCard, Visa
BREAKFAST	Full breakfast served in dining room includes juice, fruit, entree, meat, coffee, tea and milk.
AMENITIES	Heated spa with view, private entrances, TV in rooms and guided nature walk (small charge.)
RESTRICTIONS	No smoking, no pets, all children are welcome.
MEMBER	Sedona Bed & Breakfast Innkeepers Guild

LANTERN LIGHT INN

3085 West Highway 89A, Sedona, AZ 86336   *502-282-3419*
Ed & Kris Varjean, Resident Owners

THE LODGE AT SEDONA

125 Kallof Place, Sedona, AZ 86336   *520-204-1942*
Barb & Mark Dinunzio, Resident Owners   *800-619-4467*
    FAX 520-204-2128

KUDOS/COMMENTS "Comfortable and cozy."

TERRITORIAL HOUSE, AN OLD WEST B&B

65 Piki Drive, Sedona, AZ 86336
John & Linda Steele, Resident Owners

520-204-2737
800-801-2737
FAX 520-204-2230

LOCATION	3.1 miles west from Highway 89A/179 junction in Sedona, then .2 miles north on Dry Creek Road, then .4 miles west on Kachina, then left on Piki to second property on the left.
OPEN	All year
DESCRIPTION	A two-story 1975 Western ranch house with Territorial furnishings.
NO. OF ROOMS	Four rooms with private bathrooms. John suggests a room called Red Rock Crossing.
RATES	Year-round rates are $75 to $140 for a single or a double with a private bathroom.The suite is $170. There is a minimum stay on weekends and holidays and cancellation requires seven days notice.
CREDIT CARDS	Amex, MasterCard, Visa
BREAKFAST	Full breakfast is served in the dining room.
AMENITIES	Outdoor hot tub, TV and phones available, large Great Room with fireplace.
RESTRICTIONS	No smoking, no pets.
REVIEWED	*American Historic Inns, Best Places to Stay in the Southwest*
MEMBER	Professional Association of Innkeepers International, Sedona Bed & Breakfast Guild
RATED	AAA 3 Diamonds
KUDOS/COMMENTS	"Very friendly and comfortable."… "Exceptionally clean, great innkeepers, beautiful property and rooms."

A TOUCH OF SEDONA

595 Jordan Road, Sedona, AZ 86336   *520-282-6462*
Bill & Sharon Larsen, Resident Owners   *FAX 520-282-1534*

LOCATION	Corner of Jordan Road and Navahopi in uptown Sedona.
OPEN	All year
DESCRIPTION	1989 California ranch with eclectic furnishings and Southwestern themes.
NO. OF ROOMS	Five rooms with private bathrooms. Bill suggests the Roadrunner as the best room in the house.
RATES	Year-round rates for a single or a double with a private bathroom are $89 to $139. There is a minimum stay on weekends and holidays and cancellation requires seven days notice.
CREDIT CARDS	MasterCard, Visa
BREAKFAST	Full breakfast is served in the dining room and includes fresh fruit, fresh baked goodies, muffins or breads and hot gourmet entrees. A Thanksgiving meal is also available.
AMENITIES	Cable TV, 24 hour snacks and beverages, health club privileges, library, concierge service.
RESTRICTIONS	No smoking
REVIEWED	*Hidden Southwest, Fodor's - The Southwest, Non-Smoker's Guide to Bed & Breakfast*
MEMBER	Arizona Association of Bed & Breakfast Inns, American Bed & Breakfast Association, Sedona Bed & Breakfast Innkeepers Guild
RATED	AAA 3 Diamonds, ABBA 3 Crowns

STRAWBERRY

This tiny village in awesome surroundings sits just below the Mogollon Rim, 19 miles north of Payson via Highway 87. Look for wild strawberries, check out the old pioneer log schoolhouse and Tonto Natural Bridge.

STRAWBERRY HOUSE

HC1 Box 604, Strawberry, AZ 85540   *520-476-2450*

TOMBSTONE

This was "The Town Too Tough to Die," Arizona's most famous old mining camp and a National Historic Site. Guns still blaze during regular shootouts at the O.K. Corral and Allen Street. Relive the wild west during Helldorado Days in October. Visit Boothill Graveyard and The Bird Cage Theater. From Tucson, 65 miles south via I-10 and Highway 80

BUFORD HOUSE BED & BREAKFAST

---

113 East Safford Street, Tombstone, AZ 85638　　　　　520-457-3969
Brenda Reger, Resident Owner　　　　　　　　　　　　800-263-6762

LOCATION	In Tombstone midway between Boothill Cemetery and the Bird Cage Theater.
OPEN	All year
DESCRIPTION	A two-story 1880 adobe with antique furnishings; listed on both the National and State Historic Registers.
NO. OF ROOMS	Two rooms with private bathrooms and three rooms with sinks share two bathrooms. Brenda suggests the Garden Room.
RATES	Year-round rates for a single or a double with a private bathroom are $75 to $95, and a single or a double with a shared bathroom is $65. There is no minimum stay and cancellation requires 48 hours notice.
CREDIT CARDS	No
BREAKFAST	Full breakfast is served in the dining room and includes juice, fruit, eggs, sausage, ham, muffins or apple upsidedowns and French toast. Special meals are available with advanced notice.
AMENITIES	Flowers, fruit and candy in each room, BBQ area, coffee and tea anytime, board games, "But never a TV!!"...we are with you, Brenda...TI
RESTRICTIONS	No smoking indoors, no pets, children over five are welcome. The resident cats are Puffer, T.C., and Misty, the gold fish are too numerous to mention and the musician ghost hasn't announced his name yet.
REVIEWED	*Fodor's - The Southwest*

PRISCILLA'S BED & BREAKFAST

101 North Third Street, Tombstone, AZ 85638   520-457-3844
Barbara Arters, Innkeeper
Spanish spoken

LOCATION	One block north of the O.K. Corral.
OPEN	All year
DESCRIPTION	A 1904 two-story Victorian with country Victorian furnishings.
NO. OF ROOMS	Three rooms share one bathroom. Ask for the large room.
RATES	Year-round rates for a single or a double with a shared bathroom are $39 to $55. There is no minimum stay.
CREDIT CARDS	No
BREAKFAST	Full breakfast is served in the dining room and includes bacon, sausage, eggs, pancakes, homemade jam, coffee, tea and juice. "We are known for our FULL breakfast."
AMENITIES	Garden and yard.
RESTRICTIONS	No smoking upstairs in bedrooms.

TOMBSTONE BOARDING HOUSE BED & BREAKFAST

108 North 4th Street, Tombstone, AZ 85638   520-457-3716
Shirley Villarin, Resident Owner   FAX 520-457-3038

LOCATION	From I-10 take Highway 80 which goes through Tombstone, turn north on 4th Street, the B&B is on the right side in the second block.
OPEN	All year
DESCRIPTION	Two side-by-side 1880s Territorial adobes with antique furnishings.
NO. OF ROOMS	Seven rooms with private bathrooms. Choose the Red Room as the best.
RATES	Year-round rates for a single or a double with a private bathroom are $55 to $70. There is no minimum stay and cancellation requires seven days notice and a $10 fee.
CREDIT CARDS	No
BREAKFAST	Full breakfast is served in the dining room and includes juice, fruit, bacon, eggs, potatoes, biscuits or muffins.
AMENITIES	Complimentary drinks
RESTRICTIONS	No smoking

TUBAC

Home of the Tubac Presidio State Historic Park 43 miles south of Tucson on I-19.

TUBAC COUNTRY INN

13 Burruell Street, Tubac, AZ 85646   520-398-3178
James & Ruth Goebel, Resident Owners
Some Spanish spoken

LOCATION	Take exit 40 from I-19 and follow freeway side road to the Plaza, go straight ahead two blocks to Burruell, the inn is on the NE corner.
OPEN	All year except for part of August.
DESCRIPTION	A 1904 restored two-story Mercantile with Southwestern and antique furnishings. On the National and State Historic Registers.
NO. OF ROOMS	Four rooms with private bathrooms.
RATES	Year-round rates for a single or a double with a private bathroom are $65 to $85. There is no minimum stay and cancellation requires seven days notice.
CREDIT CARDS	No
BREAKFAST	Continental breakfast is served in the guestrooms and includes cereal, milk, juice, homemade breads (banana, apple-cinnamon, pumpkin), fruit, coffee and tea.
AMENITIES	TV/VCR if requested, margaritas and wine if requested, full kitchen in two suites, owner has knowledge of local golf courses, bird watching…watch out for owners with low handicaps, you could end up serving breakfast…TI
RESTRICTIONS	No smoking inside room, no pets, children over three are welcome. The resident dog is called Tricky Coyote. The owners claim that Tricky Coyote comes from "a rare Chinese mother — father from a nice neighborhood", and don't forget Buger the calico cat.

TUBAC SECRET GARDEN INN

13 Placita de Anza, Tubac, AZ 85646   520-398-9371
Don & Leila Pearsall, Resident Owners

LOCATION	In Tubac's historic zone, one block north of St. Ann's Church.
OPEN	All year
DESCRIPTION	A 1978/1992 Spanish Colonial with Southwestern and Mexican furnishings.
NO. OF ROOMS	Two rooms with private bathrooms. Leila likes room #1.
RATES	High season, October through April, rates for a single or a double with a private bathroom are $75 and low season, May through September, rates for a single or a double with a private bathroom are $65. There is a minimum stay on weekends and cancellation "on a case by case basis." ...interesting idea for cancellation policy that seems to place the guest ahead of arbitrary rules...TI
CREDIT CARDS	No
BREAKFAST	Continental breakfast is served and includes fruit, juice, large muffin and coffee.
AMENITIES	TV/VCR in rooms.
RESTRICTIONS	No smoking, no pets.
REVIEWED	Newly opened in 1994.

VALLE VERDE RANCH B&B

2149 East Frontage Road, Tubac, AZ 85640   520-398-2246
Alexandra de Mohrenschildt   FAX 520-398-2246
and Giorgio Miola, Resident Owners
Spanish, French, Italian, German spoken.

LOCATION	A quarter mile south of Tubac.
OPEN	All year
DESCRIPTION	A 1937 Mission style home furnished with antiques.
NO. OF ROOMS	Three rooms with private bathrooms.
RATES	High season, December through April, rates for a single or a double with a private bathroom are $80 to $125 and low season, May through December, rates for a single or a double with a private bathroom are $70 to $115. There is no minimum stay and cancellation requires 15 days notice and a $10 fee.
CREDIT CARDS	Amex, Diners Club, Discover, MasterCard, Visa
BREAKFAST	Full breakfast is served in the dining room and includes juice, fresh fruit, coffee, tea, eggs, French toast, bacon, sausage and breads.
AMENITIES	Flowers, TV/VCR, hot tub, hors d'oeuvres
RESTRICTIONS	No smoking, no pets, no children. The resident dog is called Nipper and Chief the horse is 32 years old.

TUCSON

Home of the University of Arizona, the "Old Pueblo" is a cosmopolitan, culturally active community, 120 miles southwest of Phoenix via I-10. Set in a high desert valley, surrounded by four major mountain ranges, it is the gateway to Saguaro National Monument. It's also a major center for astronomy with 45 telescopes in operation. Visit Flandrau Planetarium and have a cosmic experience at Kitt Peak National Observatory, 56 miles southwest via Highways 86 and 386.

CAR-MAR'S SOUTHWEST BED & BREAKFAST

6766 West Oklahoma Street, Tucson, AZ 85746   *520-578-1730*
Carol Martinez, Resident Owner

LOCATION	Drive west on Ajo from I-19, 7.1 miles to Camino Verde, go north one block to Old Ajo Road, east a half block to Camino Verde North and go two blocks to Oklahoma Street.
OPEN	All year
DESCRIPTION	A 1980 Territorial with Southwestern furnishings, on 2.5 acres.
NO. OF ROOMS	Two rooms with private bathrooms and two rooms share one bathroom. Carol picks Loree's Room as her best.
RATES	High season, January through April, rates for a single or a double with a private bathroom are $115 to $125 and rates for a single or a double with a shared bathroom are $65 to $95. Low season, May through August, rates for a single or a double with a private bathroom are $97.75 to $106.25 and rates for a single or a double with a shared bathroom are $55.25 to $80.75. There is no minimum stay and cancellation requires two weeks notice.
CREDIT CARDS	MasterCard, Visa
BREAKFAST	Full breakfast is served in the dining room and includes a variety that might include Cinnamon French toast, scrambled eggs, bacon, fresh fruit, muffins, coffee, tea and juice.
AMENITIES	Robes, baked goodies, candlelight on request, flashlights in every room, TVs, VCRs, hot tub, pool, private courtyards and patios.
RESTRICTIONS	No smoking, no pets. The two outside dogs are Dutchess and Spanky and the cat is Kit-Kat.
MEMBER	Professional Association of Innkeepers International, National Bed & Breakfast Association.
RATED	AAA 3 Diamonds

CASA ALEGRE BED & BREAKFAST

316 East Speedway Boulevard, Tucson, AZ 85705   *520-628-1800*
Phyllis Florek, Resident Owner   *800-628-5654*
Some Spanish spoken   *FAX 520-792-1880*

LOCATION	Exit from I-10 at Speedway Boulevard, travel east one mile to the corner of Speedway and 5th Avenue. The inn is on the southeast corner in the West University Historic Neighborhood.
OPEN	All year
DESCRIPTION	A 1915 Craftsman Bungalow with early 1900s antique furnishings.
NO. OF ROOMS	Four rooms with private bathrooms. Pick Saguaro.
RATES	High season, September through May, rates for a single or a double with a private bathroom are $70 to $95. The entire B&B rents for $300. Off season, June through August, rates for a single or a double with a private bathroom are $50 to $70. The entire B&B rents for $200. There is no minimum stay and cancellation requires seven days notice.
CREDIT CARDS	Discover, MasterCard, Visa
BREAKFAST	Full breakfast is served in the dining room and includes fruit juice, fresh fruit, hot entree, breakfast meat, freshly made muffins, coffee cake, hot coffee and teas.
AMENITIES	Hot tub, swimming pool, robes, large towels, patio and garden, wedding, reception and meeting facilities available, off-street parking.
RESTRICTIONS	No smoking, no pets, children welcome in the rooms that will accommodate them.
REVIEWED	*Fodor's - The Southwest, Best Places to Stay in the Southwest*
MEMBER	Arizona Bed & Breakfast Association
RATED	AAA 2 Diamonds, Mobil 2 Stars
KUDOS/COMMENTS	"Charming inn near the university, wonderful innkeeper who is always friendly, helpful and patient."

CASA TIERRA BED & BREAKFAST INN

11155 West Calle Pima, Tucson, AZ 85743   520-578-3058
Karen Hymer-Thompson   FAX 520-578-3058
Slight Spanish spoken

LOCATION	Speedway Boulevard west over Gates Pass, turn right onto Kinney Road, go .6 mile to entrance of Desert Museum and go past museum 1.2 miles, the road curves left onto Mile Wide Road. Go 1.5 miles, turn left at mail boxes and go .5 mile on dirt road, go right at fork, then go .2 mile and turn left, go .5 mile to second house on the right.
OPEN	September 1 through May 31
DESCRIPTION	A 1989 Mexican style adobe with Southwestern furnishings.
NO. OF ROOMS	Three rooms with private bathrooms. Pick Dos.
RATES	Year round rates for a single or a double with a private bathroom are $75 to $95. There is a minimum stay or additional $10 charge for a one night stand and cancellation requires seven days notice.
CREDIT CARDS	No
BREAKFAST	Full breakfast is served in the dining room, guestroom or courtyard and includes vegetarian entrees, fresh fruit, baked goods, juice, coffee, and tea.
AMENITIES	Hot tub in secluded desert area.
RESTRICTIONS	No smoking, no pets, children over three are welcome. The dogs are Rothko and Blanca, the tortoise is E.Z and the Iguana is Tito…the best Iguana name in Arizona…TI
REVIEWED	*America's Wonderful Little Hotels & Inns, Fodor - The Southwest, Best Places to Stay in the Southwest, The Birders Travel Guide*
MEMBER	Arizona Association of Bed & Breakfast Inns
RATED	AAA 2 Diamonds
KUDOS/COMMENTS	"The ultimate desert experience - a dream home in the middle of the Sonoran Desert - super breakfast." … "Great southwest ambience in secluded setting."

COPPER BELL BED & BREAKFAST

25 North Westmoreland Avenue, Tucson, AZ 85745   520-629-9929
Gertrude M. Eich, Resident Owner
German and French Spoken

LOCATION	At the base of "A" Mountain, half mile west of downtown & St. Mary's Hospital
OPEN	All year
DESCRIPTION	1902 Renovated Lava Stone with antique furnishings. On the National Historic Register.
NO. OF ROOMS	Five rooms with private bathrooms and four rooms share four bathrooms. Pick the Honeymoon Suite as the best in the house.
RATES	High season, September through April, rates for a single or a double with a private or shared bathroom are $65, the Suite is $85. Off season, May through August, rates are 10% less. There is a two night minimum stay and cancellation requires five days notice.
CREDIT CARDS	No
BREAKFAST	Full German breakfast is served and includes coffee or tea, juice, fruit salad, German bread, homemade marmalade and waffles, cheese, vegetable soup and eggs. Dinner is available by prior arrangement.
AMENITIES	Bathrobes, TV, flowers, complimentary tea and cakes.
RESTRICTIONS	Smoking limited, no pets, children over 10 are welcome. There are three resident cats, Risty, Rio and Mietze.

EL PRESIDIO BED & BREAKFAST INN

297 North Main Avenue, Tucson, AZ 85701   520-623-6151
Patti & Jerry Toci, Resident Owners

FORD'S BED & BREAKFAST

1202 North Avenida Marlene, Tucson, AZ 85715   520-885-1202
Tom & Sheila Ford, Resident Owners

THE GABLE HOUSE

2324 North Madelyn Circle, Tucson, AZ 85712   520-326-4846
Albert & Phyllis Cummings, Resident Owner   800-756-4846

LOCATION	Six miles east of I-10 on Grant Road.
OPEN	All year
DESCRIPTION	A 1930 Santa Fe pueblo with southwestern furnishings.
NO. OF ROOMS	Two rooms with private bathroom and two rooms share one bathroom. Pick Santa Maria.
RATES	Year-round rates for a single or a double with a private bathroom are $75 to $95 and a single or a double with a shared bathroom is $55 to $70. There is no minimum stay and cancellation requires 10 days notice with a $10 fee.
CREDIT CARDS	MasterCard, Visa
BREAKFAST	Continental Plus is served in the dining room and includes coffee, tea, juice, rolls, muffins, bagels, fruit, yogurt, toast hot & cold cereal.
AMENITIES	TV, telephones, robes, hot-tub spa.
RESTRICTIONS	No smoking, no pets, children over 10 are welcome. There is one outside cat.

HIDEAWAY B&B

4344 East Poe Street, Tucson, AZ 85711   520-323-8067
Ola & Dwight Parker, Resident Owners

HORIZONS

5050 North Indian Horse Trail, Tucson, AZ 85749　　　520-749-2955
Sallie Sperling, Resident Owner　　　　　　　　　　　800-723-2955
French spoken　　　　　　　　　　　　　　　　FAX 520-749-8876

LOCATION	Northeast foothills, eight miles from Tanque Verde Road and Catalina Highway.
OPEN	All year
DESCRIPTION	A 1991 contemporary Southwestern with southwestern furnishings.
NO. OF ROOMS	One suite with private bathroom.
RATES	Year-round rates for a single or a double are $101. There is no minimum stay and cancellation requires seven days notice.
CREDIT CARDS	No
BREAKFAST	Full breakfast is served in the dining room and includes baked pancakes with lingonberries, fresh fruit, bacon, coffee, tea and juice.
AMENITIES	Swimming pool, robes, Telephone, TV/VCR, canyon hiking, wildlife, views of Tucson.
RESTRICTIONS	No smoking, no pets, children over seven are welcome.
REVIEWED	*Fodor's - The Southwest*

JANE COOPER HOUSE

710 North Sixth Avenue, Tucson, AZ 85705   520-791-9677
Nancy Carlson, Resident Owner
Some Spanish and French spoken.

LOCATION	Turn off I-10 at Broadway exit, go under I-10 (left) into town, after a few blocks turn left on 6th Avenue. The B&B is between 4th Street and University Boulevard.
OPEN	October 1 through April 30
DESCRIPTION	A two-story 1905 fired red brick with two guesthouses, all with traditional furnishings.
NO. OF ROOMS	Three rooms with private bathrooms, and two rooms share one bathroom. Pick the Red Suite.
RATES	Year-round rates for a single or a double with a private bathroom are $65 to $75, for a single or a double with a shared bathroom the rates are $55 to $60, the suite and guesthouses are $65. There is no minimum stay and cancellation requires seven days notice, no refund between 1/28 and 2/15.
CREDIT CARDS	Amex, Diners Club, Discover, MasterCard, Visa
BREAKFAST	Full breakfast is served in the dining room and includes fresh juice, granola, yogurt fruiti and "then I choose what I want to cook" such as eggs benedict, German apple pancakes, fritata, etc.
AMENITIES	Telephones, cable TV, flowers, candy.
RESTRICTIONS	No smoking, no pets
REVIEWED	*Fodor's - the Southwest*

JUNE'S BED & BREAKFAST

3212 West Holladay Street, Tucson, AZ 85746   520-578-0857
June Henderson, Resident Owner

KATY'S HACIENDA

5841 East 9th Street, Tucson, AZ 85711   520-745-5695
Kate Gage, Resident Owner

LOCATION   Coming west on I-10 take the Kolb Street exit and go north to
                      Broadway, turn left and proceed two miles. Take the first right past
                      the Ogden Theater which is Chantilly, 9th Street is the next street,
                      turn right.

OPEN   All year

DESCRIPTION   An adobe cottage.

NO. OF ROOMS   One room with a private bathroom and one room shares one
                      bathroom. Pick the room with the private bathroom.

RATES   High season, October through April, rates for a single or a double
                      with a private or shared bathroom are $55. Off season, May through
                      September, rates are 10% lower.

CREDIT CARDS   No

BREAKFAST   Full breakfast of choice is served in the dining room.

AMENITIES   "Just a good, clean house. TV in each bedroom and a radio. Nothing
                      elaborate."

RESTRICTIONS   Children over 10 are welcome. The resident Chow is Chang and the
                      cat is Tillie.

REVIEWED   *Bed & Breakfast USA*

LA POSADA DEL VALLE

1640 North Campbell Avenue, Tucson, AZ 85719	520-795-3840
Tom & Karin Dennen, Resident Owners	FAX 520-795-3840
German spoken	

LOCATION	Take Speedway Boulevard exit from I-10, travel east on Speedway to Campbell Avenue, go north on Campbell to Elm Street.
OPEN	All year
DESCRIPTION	1929 Santa Fe adobe with antique, art deco furnishings.
NO. OF ROOMS	Five rooms with private bathrooms. Pick Sophies.
RATES	High season, September through May, rates for a single or a double with a private bathroom are $90 to $125 and the guesthouse is $125. Off season, June through August, rates for a single or a double with a private bathroom are $65 to $95 and the guesthouse is $95. There is no minimum stay and cancellation requires 14 days notice and a $10 fee.
CREDIT CARDS	MasterCard, Visa
BREAKFAST	Full breakfast is served on the weekends and Continental Plus is served weekdays in the dining room and includes fresh fruit, juice, yogurts, cereals, breakfast breads or muffins.
AMENITIES	Phone, TV, library and private parking.
RESTRICTIONS	No smoking, no pets, children over 12 are welcome. Chico the dog is "very entertaining."
REVIEWED	*Arizona Traveler's Handbook, Best Places to Stay in the Southwest*
MEMBER	Arizona Association of Bed & Breakfast Inns, Professional Association of Innkeepers International
RATED	AAA 3 Diamonds, Mobil 3 Stars

THE LODGE ON THE DESERT

306 North Alvernon Way, Tucson, AZ 85711
Shirley Evans, General Manager
Spanish, some German and French spoken

520-325-3366
800-456-5634
Fax 520-327-5834

LOCATION	From I-10 take Speedway exit right on Alvernon Way. The lodge is on the left between 5th Street and Broadway on Alvernon.
OPEN	All year
DESCRIPTION	A 1936 Spanish Hacienda with Southwestern furnishings.
NO. OF ROOMS	40 adobe colored casas with private bathrooms grouped around patios. Ask for the room with the private swimming pool.
RATES	High season, November 1 through May 31, rates for a single or a double with a private bathroom are $82 to $177 and suites are $111 to $139. Off season, June 1 through October 31, rates for a single or a double with a private bathroom are $56 to $134 and suites are $74 to $94. There in no minimum stay and there is a cancellation policy.
CREDIT CARDS	Amex, Carte Blanche, Diners Club, MasterCard, Visa
BREAKFAST	Continental, served in dining or guest rooms, other meals and catering available.
AMENITIES	TV, telephone, meeting facilities for up to 45, some handicapped accessible rooms.
RESTRICTIONS	None
MEMBER	Independent Innkeepers Association

MELISSA'S BED & BREAKFAST

7400 North Juniper Road, Tucson, AZ 85741
Jane Madden, Resident Owner

520-744-1984

PAZ ENTERA BED,
BREAKFAST & BEYOND

7501 North Wade Road, Tucson, AZ 85743   *520-744-2481*
Glenn & Molli Nickell, Resident Owners

LOCATION	I-10 exit at Ina Road, go three miles west to Wade Road, ranch is .3 mile north on Wade.
OPEN	All year
DESCRIPTION	1930s two-story adobe guest ranch with southwestern furnishings; located on 30 acres.
NO. OF ROOMS	Ten rooms with private bathrooms. Pick Suite 8B.
RATES	High season, November through May, rates for a single or a double with a private bathroom are $85 to $95, and suites are $120 to $130. Off season, June through October, rates for a single or a double with a private bathroom are $75 to $85 and suite are $110 to $120. The entire B&B rents for $2,000. There is a minimum stay on holidays and during the Gem Show in February and cancellation requires 10 days notice.
CREDIT CARDS	Amex, Diners Club, Discover, MasterCard, Visa
BREAKFAST	Continental Plus is served in the dining room and includes fresh fruit, juices, yogurt, Danish, hot and cold cereal, cocoa, coffee, teas, bagels, breads, hard-boiled eggs, granola. Special meals can be catered.
AMENITIES	Gazebo-covered Jacuzzi, hammocks, wildlife on property and meeting rooms.
RESTRICTIONS	No smoking, no pets, children over 10 are welcome. Mongoose the cat is an expert snake and mouse catcher.

THE PEPPERTREES
BED & BREAKFAST INN

724 East University Boulevard, Tucson, AZ 85719   520-622-7167
Marjorie G. Martin, Resident Owner   800-348-5763
Spanish and French spoken.   FAX 520-622-5959

LOCATION
From I-10 take Speedway .7 mile to the University of Arizona, turn right on Stone Avenue and go three blocks to University and turn left. The inn is seven blocks on the right.

OPEN
All year

DESCRIPTION
1905 red brick Victorian and guesthouse with antique and Southwestern furnishings, wood floors and Oriental carpets.

NO. OF ROOMS
Three rooms with private bathrooms and two rooms in the guest house share one bathroom. Marjorie says that Jamy's room is the best in the house.

RATES
High season, September through June, rates for a single or a double with a private bathroom are $78 to $88; the guesthouse rents for $150 and the entire inn rents for $565. Off season, June through August, rates for a single or a double with a private bathroom are $60 to $75 and the guesthouse rents for $120. There is a two-night minimum stay on holiday weekends and cancellation requires seven days notice.

CREDIT CARDS
Discover, MasterCard, Visa

BREAKFAST
Full breakfast is served in the dining room or on the patio and includes fruit, cereal, yogurt, main dish, breads, homemade scones, muffins, jams and syrups.

AMENITIES
Robes in guesthouse, TV in living rooms, phone, and library information on what to do and where to go.

RESTRICTIONS
No smoking, no pets, children are welcome in the guesthouse only. The resident Lab/Retriever mix is called Shelby Underfoot...Best B&B dog name in Arizona...TI

REVIEWED
Fodor's - The Southwest, Ultimate Arizona, America's Wonderful Little Hotels & Inns: Rocky Mountains and the Southwest.

MEMBER
Professional Association of Innkeepers International, Arizona Association of Bed & Breakfast Inns

RATED
AAA 3 Diamonds

KUDOS/COMMENTS
"Very nice, clean, good breakfast"

Quail's Vista Bed & Breakfast

826 East Palisades Drive, Tucson, AZ 85737　　　　　520-297-5980
Barbara Jones, Resident Owner

LOCATION	Northwest of Tucson in the town of Ono Valley. From I-10 exit on Tangerine and go east 12 miles to a four-way stop at 1st Avenue, then south to Palisades, east on Palisades to four mail boxes, turn right on driveway to 2nd house.
OPEN	All year
DESCRIPTION	A 1989 passive solar rammed earth adobe on two acres with eclectic furnishings.
NO. OF ROOMS	One master suite and two rooms share one bathroom. Pick the Master Suite.
RATES	Year-round rates for the suite with a private bathroom are $85 and a single or a double with a shared bathroom is $65. There in no minimum stay and cancellation requires two weeks notice.
CREDIT CARDS	No
BREAKFAST	Continental Plus is served in the kitchen or "living room to watch birds" and includes five cereals, three juices, milk, bagels, bread, sweet rolls, coffee and tea.
AMENITIES	Master suite has fireplace and hot tub, TV and telephone, living room has TV, fireplace, VCR and piano.
RESTRICTIONS	Smoking outside only, no pets, children over eight are welcome. The dogs who, "like to be held by everyone" are called Misty (7 lbs.) and Gidget (8 lbs.).
REVIEWED	*Fodor's - The Southwest*

Rancho Quieto

12051 West Fort Lowell Road, Tucson, AZ 85743　　　　　520-883-3300
Corinne Still, Resident Owner

KUDOS/COMMENTS	"Very Comfortable, very lovely" … "Great remote hideaway in a perfect setting."

REDBUD HOUSE BED & BREAKFAST

7002 East Redbud Road, Tucson, AZ 85715   *520-721-0218*
Kenneth & Wanda Mayer, Resident Owners
A little German and Polish spoken

LOCATION	From Grant Road exit of I-10 go east about 10 miles to Tanque Verde Road, turn left, proceed to Sabino Canyon Road, then turn left, East Redbud is a block away.
OPEN	All year
DESCRIPTION	1980 brick ranch host home with country and eclectic furnishings.
NO. OF ROOMS	One room with private bathroom.
RATES	Year-round rates for a single or a double with a private bathroom are $40 to $50. There is no minimum stay and "reasonable notice" is needed for cancellation. "Some" flexibility here...We applaud guest oriented cancellation policies...TI
CREDIT CARDS	No
BREAKFAST	Full breakfast is served in the dining room and includes a hot beverage of choice, juice, a breakfast meat, plus a main course, bread and muffins.
AMENITIES	Beverage, fruit or candy on arrival, TV, telephone on request, bicycles, newspaper, BBQ grill on the patio, message service.
RESTRICTIONS	No smoking, no pets, no children.
MEMBER	Tourist Home Association of America

RIMROCK WEST HACIENDA

3450 North Drake Place, Tucson, AZ 85749   520-749-8774
Mae & Val Robbins, Resident Owners
Spanish spoken

LOCATION	From the airport, go right on Valencia and then left on Alvernon Way, bear left on Golf Links and turn left on Wilmot that becomes Tanque Verde. Go left on Catalina Highway, then right one mile on Prince to Rimrock.
OPEN	September 1 through May 30
DESCRIPTION	1960 Southwestern adobe hacienda and cottage on 20 acres with southwestern furnishings
NO. OF ROOMS	Three rooms with private bathrooms in the main house and one adobe guesthouse with private bathroom, sunken living room, fireplace, complete kitchen & private patio.
RATES	Seasonal rates for a single or a double with a private bathroom are $95. The cottage rents for $140. There is a two night minimum stay and a cancellation policy.
CREDIT CARDS	No
BREAKFAST	Full breakfast is served in the dining room or in the courtyard and includes fresh brewed coffee, tea, blended fruit juice, omelettes, pancakes, waffles, souffles and Mae's special muffins...a field report on the muffins please...TI
AMENITIES	Outdoor swimming pool, TV/radio in rooms; hot or cold tea with cookies on arrival.
RESTRICTIONS	No smoking, no pets and children over 16 are welcome. The resident Lhasa Apso goes by the name of Kittie.
REVIEWED	*America's Wonderful Little Hotels & Inns*
MEMBER	American Bed & Breakfast Association

THE SUNCATCHER

105 North Avenida Javalina, Tucson, AZ 85748   520-885-0883
David Williams & Keith Waterbrook, Resident Owners   800-835-8012

TUMACACORI

Home of the world famous Tumacacori National Monument this village is 18 miles north of the Mexican border on I-19

THE OLD MISSION STORE
BED & BREAKFAST

1908 East Frontage Road, Tumacacori, AZ 85640   520-398-9583
Kim & David Yubeta, Resident Owners
Spanish spoken

LOCATION	Forty five miles south of Tucson, exit #34 from I-19, go south on East Frontage Road to Tumacacori, next to Post Office.
OPEN	All year
DESCRIPTION	A 1926 Territorial adobe with Western and Mexican furnishings.
NO. OF ROOMS	One room with private bathroom.
RATES	Year-round rates for a single or a double with a private bathroom are $55 to $65. There is no minimum stay.
CREDIT CARDS	No
BREAKFAST	Full breakfast is served in the sitting room of the suite and includes sausage and green chili quiche, fresh fruit bowl, fresh squeezed orange juice, homemade muffins, coffee and tea.
AMENITIES	TV in bedroom, refrigerator stocked with complimentary beer, wine soda and mineral water, flannel sheets, fresh flowers.
RESTRICTIONS	No smoking, no pets—"negotiable, will accept small dogs with no teeth"...best kind of small dog...TI. Buddy the cat, "thinks every guest has come to see him."...typical cat...TI
KUDOS/COMMENTS	"Much character and charm."

WICKENBURG

This old mining town is a winter resort and dude ranch country, 58 miles northwest of Phoenix via Highway 60/89, or I-17 and Highway 74. Check out the Hassayampa River Preserve, Gold Rush Days in February and the Bluegrass Festival in November.

J BAR J RANCH

Rincon Road, Wickenburg, AZ 85358   520-684-9142
Janice & J.J. Fletcher, Resident Owners   FAX 520-684-0202
Chinese spoken

LOCATION	From Wickenburg go north two miles on Highway 90, turn right (east) on Rincon Road and go one mile to river where the paved road ends, cross the river and 1.8 miles, "y'all have arrived."
OPEN	All year
DESCRIPTION	A 1994 hacienda with Southwestern cowboy furnishings.
NO. OF ROOMS	Five rooms with private bathrooms.
RATES	Year-round rates for a single or a double with a private bathroom are $65. There is a minimum stay during Gold Rush Days in February and the Bluegrass Festival in November. Cancellation requires 24 hours notice.
CREDIT CARDS	No
BREAKFAST	Full "gourmet breakfast with several courses" is served in the dining room and special meals are available by special arrangement.
AMENITIES	Horse boarding, custom trail rides.
RESTRICTIONS	No smoking, pets require advance notice and the ranch is "not really suitable for children." There are "lots" of horses, four to seven ranch dogs and barn cats.
REVIEWED	*North American Horse Travel Guide*

Rincon Ranch Lodge

Rincon Ranch Road, Wickenburg, AZ 85358   520-684-2328
Ken & Betty Park Gibson, Resident Owners   FAX 520-684-2328

LOCATION	Three miles north from the center of Wickenburg on Highways 93 and 89, on Rincon Road 1.4 miles the last .8 miles is rural dirt road.
OPEN	November 1 through May 31
DESCRIPTION	A 1920-1970 ranch headquarters with cabins furnished with Georgian antiques.
NO. OF ROOMS	Five rooms with private bathrooms. Choose the Guest Room as the best in the house.
RATES	Year-round rates for a single or a double with a private bathroom are $60. There is no minimum stay and there is a cancellation policy.
CREDIT CARDS	Inquire
BREAKFAST	Full breakfast is served in the dining room and includes pancakes, toast, breakfast bread, meat, eggs, juice, fruit and cereal on request.
AMENITIES	Wine in rooms, no TV or telephone (available in main lodge), horse boarding, horseback riding, dinner rides, cook outs, fireplace, gameroom and piano in lodge.
RESTRICTIONS	No smoking, no pets, no children. There are 40 horses on the property and the resident Australian Shepherd is called Lady Bug.

Vista del Oro

56851 North Vulture Mine Road, Wickenburg, AZ 85358   520-684-3991
Roxie & Rome Glover, Resident Owners

WILLIAMS

This "Gateway to the Grand Canyon" is 58 miles west of Flagstaff via I-40, and a straight shot to the park via Highway 64. Or steam out of Williams aboard the Grand Canyon Railway's authentically-restored, turn of the century trains. Ski at Bill Williams Mountain. Check out the Deer Farm, Bill Williams Rendezvous Days in May, and outdoor fun and fishing at White Horse, Kaibab and Cataract Lakes.

THE JOHNSTONIAN BED & BREAKFAST

321 West Sheridan Avenue, Williams, AZ 86046   *520-635-2178*
Bill & Pidge Johnston, Resident Owners

LOCATION	About one mile south of I-40 exit 163 or three blocks south of the main one-way street (Bill Williams Avenue) through Williams.
OPEN	All year
DESCRIPTION	1990 two-story Victorian with antique furnishings and floral wall coverings.
NO. OF ROOMS	One room with private bathroom and three rooms share one bathroom.
RATES	Year-round rates for a single or a double with a private bathroom are $60 to $65 and $45 to $55 for a single or a double with a shared bathroom. Suite is $108 to $110. There is no minimum stay and cancellation requires 14 days notice, 72 hours is less a $15 fee.
CREDIT CARDS	No
BREAKFAST	Full breakfast is served in the dining room and includes bacon, eggs, fruit, homemade apple sauce, fruit juices, hot drinks, homebaked bread.
AMENITIES	TV/VCR in room with private bathroom, sitting room has TV/VCR, homemade desserts served some evenings, airport or Amtrak pickups available.
RESTRICTIONS	No smoking except on front porch. The resident outside cat is called Oink who, "likes to eat."...good name for a cat...TI
REVIEWED	*Bed & Breakfast USA, Be Our Guest*

Red Garter Bed & Bakery

137 West Railroad Avenue, Williams, AZ 86046   520 635-1484
John Holst, Resident Owner

LOCATION	At the center of greater downtown Williams, across the street and a half block east of the visitor's center.
OPEN	All year, closed the month of January.
DESCRIPTION	An 1897 Romanesque Victorian with Victorian furnishings.
NO. OF ROOMS	Four rooms with private bathrooms.
RATES	High season, April through October, rates for a single or a double with a private bathroom are $45 to $65, a suite is $85 and the entire B&B rents for $250. Off season, November through March, rates for a single or a double with a private bathroom are $35 to $45, a suite is $65 and the entire B&B rents for $200. There is no minimum stay and cancellation requires 72 hours notice.
CREDIT CARDS	Amex, Discover, MasterCard, Visa
BREAKFAST	Continental breakfast is served in the dining room and includes freshly baked pastries, fruit, juices and coffee. Lunch is also available.
AMENITIES	Cable TV
RESTRICTIONS	No smoking, no pets, no children.

Terry Ranch

701 Quarterhorse Road, Williams, AZ 86046   520-635-4171
Del & Sheryl Terry, Resident Owners

Williams Canyon Country Inn

442 West Bill Williams Avenue, Williams, AZ 86046   520-635-2349
Joyce Sullivant, Resident Owner   800-643-1020

YUMA

An important agricultural area and recreation center on the Colorado and Gila Rivers and the California/Mexico border, 116 miles west of Gila Bend via I-8 and 184 miles southwest of Phoenix. Check out Yuma Crossing Day and Quartzite Pow Wow in February and World Championship Raft Race in August.

CASA DE OSGOOD BED & BREAKFAST

11620 Ironwood Drive, Yuma, AZ 85367   520-342-0471
Chris & Vickie Osgood, Resident Owners

LOCATION	Twelve miles east of Yuma, two miles off I-8 taking Foothill Boulevard exit #14.
OPEN	All year
DESCRIPTION	A 1987 Spanish country home with country furnishings.
NO. OF ROOMS	One room with private bathroom.
RATES	Year-round rates for a single or a double with a private bathroom are $65. There is no minimum stay.
CREDIT CARDS	No
BREAKFAST	Continental breakfast is served in the dining room and is "delicious, it varies."
AMENITIES	Large room with fireplace, TV, Queen bed and private patio.
RESTRICTIONS	No smoking, no pets, no children
REVIEWED	*Bed & Breakfast USA*

BED & BREAKFAST INDEX

ABOUT THE PUBLISHER

TRAVIS ILSE PUBLISHERS is a traditional trade publishing house with a slight twist. In the lexicon of business writers, Travis Ilse Publishers is a virtual corporation. There is one principal and a crew of independent free-lancers who run their own companies or work for other companies that sell their skills to Travis Ilse Publishers.

When we speak of sitting around the publishing house it might mean our bimonthly meetings in Boulder, but more than likely it means each of us sitting at a Mac in our various offices talking to each other or sending data on America On Line, working the FAX or chatting on the phone. The advantages of a virtual corporation are psychological and practical. Each of us can live exactly where we want, work when we want and be truly responsible for our own fate. Practically speaking, we are extraordinarily flexible and responsive to the marketplace. The B&B industry is volatile, but by constantly updating our databases we can revise our books every two to two-and-a-half years, making the *Absolutely Every°* series of B&B books as current as our corporation.

We are:

ALAN BERNHARD is the production manager, computer wizard and scheduler for Travis Ilse Publishers. He is the president of Argent Associates that produces books for eight other publishers; the executive director of the Rocky Mountain Book Publishers Association, and lives in Boulder with his son and daughter.

TRAVIS ILSE is the senior editor and owner of the house. He was neither caught in the 1968 Chicago police riot nor was he on the last chopper out of Saigon. He did not inhale. And while he is a conscientious letter writer, he does not return phone calls, make appointments or fly commercial airlines if he can help it. He lives in the Front Range with a younger woman and looks down on Boulder.

TONI KNAPP is the originator, editor, quality control person and half of the data entry crew. She is an editor at Roberts Rinehart Publisher. In addition to editing this series of books she has written *The Six Bridges of Humphrey the Whale*, *The Gossamer Tree* and *Ordinary Splendors: Tales of Virtues and Wisdoms*. She has a grown son and lives with her dogs in Colorado Springs.

ALAN STARK is the publisher, marketing type and half of the data entry crew. He is the owner of Bear Marketing, a free-lance marketing and sales management concern for four independent publishers in the west, and recently finished a four year term on the board of the Colorado Center for the Book. He lives in Seattle with his best friend Linda.

All of us can be reached by letter at PO Box 583, Niwot, CO 80544 or if it's urgent, at SaltyBear@aol.com. Thank you for buying our book. Write us anytime.

ORDERING INFORMATION

If you would like additional copies of this book or other books in the series, please contact your local bookstore and give her all the information listed with each title. If the bookseller doesn't have the book in stock, he can get it for you in about a week to ten days from Publishers Group West or a trade book wholesaler.

THE ROCKY MOUNTAIN SERIES

Absolutely Every° Bed & Breakfast in Arizona (°Almost), Toni Knapp, editor, ISBN 1-882092-12-0, $14.95.

Absolutely Every° Bed & Breakfast in California, Monterey to San Diego (°Almost), Toni Knapp, editor, ISBN 1-882092-10-4, $15.95

Absolutely Every° Bed & Breakfast in Northern California (°Almost), Toni Knapp, editor, ISBN 1-882092-13-9, $16.95

Absolutely Every° Bed & Breakfast in Colorado (°Almost), Toni Knapp, editor, ISBN 1-882092-08-2, $15.95

Absolutely Every° Bed & Breakfast in New Mexico (°Almost), Toni Knapp, editor, ISBN 1-882092-07-4, $12.95

Absolutely Every° Bed & Breakfast in Texas (°Almost), Toni Knapp, editor, ISBN 1-882092-15-5, $18.95

Absolutely Every° Bed & Breakfast in Washington (°Almost), Toni Knapp, editor, ISBN 1-882092-16-3, $18.95

THE MISSISSIPPI RIVER SERIES

Absolutely Every° Bed & Breakfast in Illinois (°Almost), Toni Knapp, editor, ISBN 1-882092-14-7, $15.95.